CW01431741

The Roman Catholic Bishops of Portsmouth

1882–2012

— PAUL SEVERN —

Sacristy
Press

Sacristy Press
PO Box 612, Durham, DH1 9HT

www.sacristy.co.uk

First published in 2025 by Sacristy Press, Durham

Copyright © Paul Severn 2025
The moral rights of the author have been asserted.

All rights reserved, no part of this publication may be reproduced
or transmitted in any form or by any means, electronic,
mechanical photocopying, documentary, film or in any other
format without prior written permission of the publisher.

Every reasonable effort has been made to trace the copyright holders
of material reproduced in this book, but if any have been inadvertently
overlooked the publisher would be glad to hear from them.

Sacristy Limited, registered in England & Wales, number 7565667

British Library Cataloguing-in-Publication Data
A catalogue record for the book is available from the British Library

ISBN 978-1-78959-379-2

Contents

Acknowledgements

I am indebted to a number of people and organizations who have helped me realize this text on the first seven Roman Catholic bishops of Portsmouth and the one auxiliary.

First and foremost, to the Isle of Wight Catholic History Society and its chairman, Mr Peter Clarke. Peter has helped and encouraged since I first wrote a little booklet for the Society on Bishop Cahill, in 2018. He has also made available to me many of the archives and records held by the society. More recently, Peter has continued to encourage me in my writing, and the Society also made a financial contribution to these researches, for which I am most grateful.

The English Catholic History Association has been an encouragement in my work and also made a financial contribution for which I am, again, most grateful.

I am grateful to the staff at Portsmouth Central Library, particularly the History Centre on the second floor; also to Ms Jean Watson at the Portsmouth Diocesan Archive when it was in Copnor. I am also grateful to Deacon Craig Aburn and Dr J. L. Kettle Williams who tracked down, for me, a copy of the 2012 edition of *Portsmouth People* commemorating Bishop Hollis.

I am grateful to a number of priests who have shared memories with me and responded to questions and queries, particularly Fr John Catlin and Fr Jonathan Redvers Harris.

And not least to Ray Davis, Stuart Robinson and Chris Roberts, who read through various versions of my draft text and offered many corrections and suggestions for improvement.

Finally, I am, of course, grateful to all the staff at Sacristy Press.

Introduction

Following the Reformation in England, the English Catholic dioceses died out. They existed in a theoretical sense, on paper only, and were all vacant sees without a resident bishop. The territory was considered as mission territory, *in partibus infidelium*, by Rome; and the region that is now the Diocese of Portsmouth was part of the London District, created in 1688, whose first vicar apostolic was Bishop James Leyburne (*d.*1702). In 1840, the four vicariates were increased in number to eight, but Portsmouth and the surrounding area remained in the (new) London District.

In 1766, under George III, the harsh penal laws started to be dismantled, and the First Catholic Relief Act, known as the Papists Act, was passed in 1778. The Second Relief Act of 1791 was more far-reaching than the Papists Act and (loosely) permitted the building of Catholic churches (albeit without steeples or bells) and the exercise of the Catholic religion. In 1829, the Third Catholic Relief Act (The Catholic Emancipation Act) was the conclusion of the reforms. It repealed the Test Act of 1672 and the remaining penal laws. Catholics were once again allowed to take an active part in the civic and political life of the borough and state, so that once again Roman Catholics could sit in parliament at Westminster.

These pieces of legislation are important, for they paved the way for Pope Pius IX to promulgate the Bull *Universalis Ecclesiae* in 1850 (29 September), by which the Catholic hierarchy in England and Wales was restored (the Scottish hierarchy was not restored until 1878). The London Vicariate (one of eight), previously administered by an Apostolic Vicar, became the Metropolitan Archdiocese of Westminster, and then there were a further 12 dioceses covering England and Wales. Pertinent to our story is that Portsmouth and the surrounding area fell within the Diocese of Southwark, whose first bishop was Thomas Grant (1816–70).

Having said this, it is important to remember that Catholicism in England was never completely eradicated. It continued underground, and recusant families, often based in large rural estates, sheltered heroic priests who travelled incognito from continental Europe. Many of these came from the English College at Douai in Flanders, founded by William Cardinal Allen in 1568. Indeed, it is estimated that some 450 priests had been sent to the English Mission by the end of Elizabeth I's reign in 1603. Historical records name 32 of these priests, who served in Hampshire between 1575 and 1603, and the houses in which they stayed.

From as early as 1582, Portsmouth and its surrounds had been something of a Catholic stronghold. Indeed, Hampshire had the third highest number of Catholic recusants in the country, only surpassed by Lancashire and Yorkshire.[1] One of the chief reasons for this was the faithful landed families in the area, and indeed there were significant centres of Catholicism centred round the Cotton family of Warblington Castle, the Poundes at Farlington and the Shelleys at Mapledurham.

Nonetheless, the risks incurred by both clergy and laity at the time were not insignificant and there is a number of Catholic martyrs associated with Hampshire, Berkshire and the Isle of Wight. Perhaps foremost amongst them is St Swithun Wells (c.1536–91), a country gentleman from Brambridge House in Hampshire and a onetime schoolmaster, who sheltered priests at his London house and arranged safe passage for priests travelling between Catholic households. He was arrested in 1586 and again in 1587. In 1591, Edmund Gennings was saying Mass at Wells' house when officers hunting priests burst in. Wells was arrested, and convicted under the 1585 Act "Against Jesuits, Seminary Priests and other such Disobedient Subjects". He was hanged at his own house on 10 December 1591 and buried at St Andrew's Church in Holborn. He was beatified by Pope Pius XI in 1929 and canonized by Pope Paul VI in 1970 as one of the Forty Martyrs of England and Wales.

There is quite a long list of other martyrs associated with the Diocese of Portsmouth. For example, St Edmund Campion SJ (1540–81) was arrested at Lyford Grange House (then in Berkshire, now in Oxfordshire, and falling within the diocesan boundary) while conducting Catholic ministry underground. An annual Mass in his memory is now celebrated in the barn of the old house each summer.

Two Lancashire-born men who were educated at Oxford and then went to Douai for seminary training and ordination were returning to England when they encountered a storm and their ship ran aground on the Isle of Wight. Blessed Robert Anderton and Blessed William Marsden were arrested, imprisoned for a time in London and then condemned to the punishment appointed by law and returned via Winchester to the Isle of Wight, where on 25 April 1586, having refused to recant, "on some high ground in sight of the moaning sea . . . they underwent the extreme penalty, being hanged, disembowelled and mangled".[2]

The Venerable Thomas Titchbourne, who was born at Hartley in Hampshire, was a Jesuit priest ordained at Douai. He returned to England in 1594, ministering to Catholics in secret. He was perhaps the last of the martyrs associated with the diocese and was executed on 20 April 1602.

The Catholic community in Portsmouth grew rapidly from around 150 in 1791 to over 1,000 by 1830. Having said this, the expression *in Portsmouth* is used loosely, for the 1791 Relief Act still forbade the practice of Catholicism within English incorporated boroughs and so, strictly speaking, there was no Catholicism in Portsmouth. The principal mission (as "parishes" were dubbed then) was in Portsea. A priest was appointed, and a succession of chapels was built. The first legal post-Reformation Mass was probably celebrated in the area sometime just before Christmas 1792, but the location is not known.[3] A directory of 1796 referred to a chapel at 2 Unicorn Row, and in 1807 there is a reference to a chapel in Prince George Street, Portsea under the Revd F. de la Rue. This was a considerably larger building with more seating and an adjacent "parsonage". This chapel was dedicated to St John. As this Portsea church is on Southsea Island, it is also sometimes referred to as St John's, Southsea. Finally, as Portsea / Southsea was both a centre for a military garrison and a place where people came to seek employment, the Catholic community (strengthened by the Irish!) grew rapidly.

Following the passing of the Third Relief Act and the growth of the community, it was decided that a new large church should be built in Portsmouth proper. In 1869, some redundant land was bought from the War Department for £1800 as a suitable site for the new church. In 1876, a competition was staged to find a design for a new Portsmouth parish church to be built on this land. John Crawley won the competition and building started on a new church aided by a donation of £4,000 from the Duke of Norfolk. The foundation stone was laid in 1880 by Bishop Danell of Southwark. Regrettably, Crawley died in 1881, but his work was taken over and continued under Stanislaus Hansom, son of Joseph Hansom, the designer of the famous Hansom black taxi cab. Hansom made some changes to Crawley's original design, but, in time, a church of Fareham brick and Portland stone in the French Gothic style was built with circular apse and shallow transepts.

On 19 May 1882, Pope Leo XIII issued an Apostolic Brief dividing the Diocese of Southwark and forming the new Diocese of Portsmouth out of the western part, to include Hampshire, Dorset, Berkshire, parts of south Oxfordshire, the Isle of Wight and the Channel Islands: some 6,339 square kilometres in total. Dr John Vertue was appointed as the first bishop, and the new parish church in Portsmouth became the cathedral.

Notes

[1]   Cf. Gerard Dwyer, *Diocese of Portsmouth: Past and Present* (Portsmouth: Portsmouth Diocesan Centenary Committee, 1981), p. 1.

[2]   Edwin H. Burton DD and J. H. Pollen SJ (eds), *Lives of the English Martyrs*, vol. I (London: Longman Green & Co., 1914), p. 210.

[3]   Valerie Fontana, *Rebirth of Roman Catholicism in Portsmouth* (Portsmouth: Portsmouth Papers, 1989), p. 5.

1

John Vertue (1882–1900)

John Vertue (with the variant spelling Virtue) was born on 28 April 1826 at 58 Newman Street, Holborn, London. Vertue's father was another John Vertue who was recorded in the 1861 census as a carpenter and upholsterer from Chiswick and aged 66, so we may infer he was born in 1795. He died on 12 April 1862 (aged 69), and his death was registered in the second quarter in the Kensington District. Vertue's own obituary suggests that John Vertue senior "was well-known in London Catholic circles".[1]

Bishop Vertue's mother was most probably Frances (née Fleming), an older woman, who was born in 1783. There is a record of the baptism of Frances Fleming on 14 January 1784 in Petworth, Sussex, the daughter of William and Sarah, and this rather suggests that Frances Fleming was perhaps not a Catholic, but a member of the Church of England. Further, there is a record in the registers of the marriage of a John Vertue with Frances Fleming on 17 July 1824 at St James, Westminster (i.e. St James', Piccadilly, a Church of England church). Frances Vertue's death was recorded in the fourth quarter of 1863 in the Kensington district. She did not leave a will.

Young John Vertue was first educated at Dr Kenny's (school) located at 5 Fitzroy Street, Fitzroy Square. This was a Catholic day school run by William Stopford Kenny (1788–1867), a noted author, educationalist and accomplished chess player. His son, William David Kenny, was also a schoolmaster. The *Catholic Directory and Annual Register* for 1840 makes reference to the school, noting that the boys eat with Dr Kenny and his wife and are taught manners, behaviour at table and the Catholic faith as well as "Latin, Greek, French, English languages, geography, history, writing, arithmetic &c".[2] It is perhaps notable that Kenny wrote several books, including a school textbook, *Kenny's School Geography* (1856), and if we were looking for early inspiration for Vertue's life of international travel, which was relatively unusual at the time, then it is not excessively fanciful to imagine *Kenny's School Geography* may well have been it.

In 1841, aged 16 and, we might well imagine, with a sound educational foundation, Vertue progressed from school to King's College London, which was founded by King George IV in 1829 and (along with University College London) became one of the two founding colleges of the University of London in 1836. The college archives record and confirm the information that John Vertue was the son of John Vertue (senior) resident at 58 Newman Street and born on 28 April 1825. The records tell us Vertue was admitted as a pupil in the Department of Civil Engineering and Architecture, and that assorted fees (including tuition for two terms and a cap and gown) totalling £25 6s were paid on 17 April 1841. There is no record of Vertue's graduation, but graduation was not regarded then as it is now. Students simply finished their course of study. It is worth noting that King's did not have its own charter to award degrees at the time, but that students could, if they wished, sit London University examinations and be awarded a London degree, but this incurred additional costs.

Finally, we might note that King's students often receive the award of Associate of King's College (AKC), but there is no record of Vertue having done this either. However, it is easy to understand that if by this time Vertue's mind was set on seminary and priesthood, the collection of secular qualifications was perhaps not a priority.

After King's, in 1845, Vertue went to St Edmund's College, Old Green in Ware, Hertfordshire. William Cardinal Allen founded the English College at Douai in 1568, to continue to train English men for the priesthood during penal times. Many of these ordained men subsequently returned illegally to England to minister. The work of the English College, Douai was brought to an end by the effects of the French Revolution (1789) and closed in 1793. Because the Catholic Relief Acts had made conditions for Catholics relatively safe once more, the staff and pupils returned to England, and joined the students and staff at the Old Hall Green Academy, which subsequently became St Edmund's College,

Ware. A gift of £10,000 from John Stone, a Hampshire Catholic, allowed new buildings (designed by James Taylor) to be built and a chapel by Augustus Pugin was designed and completed in 1853.

In 1849, Vertue went to Rome to continue his studies at the Venerable English College, where Dr Grant, later Bishop of Southwark, was the Rector. The Venerable English College (the *Venerabile*) was founded in 1579, by Pope Gregory XIII, as a place to train priests for the English Mission, in a building which had formerly been a hospice to accommodate English pilgrims in Rome. It was, in a sense, an overflow institution for the English College in Douai. At the time of the Reformation, it was a criminal offence to return from Europe to England as a priest, and the early life of the college was sanctified by the blood of 44 alumni who were martyred. The first of these was St Ralph Sherwin, who was martyred in 1581 alongside St Edmund Campion (feast day 1 December).

Following the restoration of the Catholic hierarchy in England in 1850, the college became "more distinguished for the production of bishops than of martyrs".[3] Cardinal Wiseman, the first Catholic Archbishop of Westminster, had been Rector of the college. Similarly, Cardinal Hinsley was Rector of the college and his successor as Rector, William Godfrey, was subsequently Apostolic Delegate in London and then Archbishop of Liverpool and Westminster. Of course, although never Rector in Rome, Bishop John Vertue was a part of this same tradition.

Vertue excelled in his studies at the *Venerabile* and was chosen to give the customary (Latin) St Stephen's Day sermon before Pope Pius IX. It is recorded that Vertue's efforts left a lasting impression. Having received minor orders, Vertue was ordained priest in Rome, for the Diocese of Westminster, on 20 December 1851 at the hands of the Italian Cardinal, Constantino Patrizi Naro (1798–1879).

In June 1852, Vertue returned to the UK to become curate at the Catholic church in Poplar under Fr Hearsulp. St Mary and St Joseph's in Poplar was established as a mission or parish in 1818, when Fr Benjamin Barber took lodgings in Hale Street. By 1819, there was a small chapel and by 1835 a larger chapel attached to the school. On account of the growing Catholic population, land was bought in Gate Street (now part of Canton Street) and work was begun on a new church in the 1840s. There were some financial difficulties, but it is recorded that Fr Vertue "worked with great energy to raise funds towards completing the church at Poplar and became well loved by the people".[4] The new church, cruciform in shape with a lantern, was 136 feet long and 80 feet wide and was said to be one of the finest in its day in London. It was completed and finally opened on 24 September 1856.

Vertue only stayed in Poplar for a year, because in June 1853 he became the secretary to Mgr Gaetano Bedini, who had recently been consecrated titular Archbishop of Thebes and Papal Emissary, and he was the first Apostolic Nuncio to the United States. Vertue travelled with him in the States, and it is probable that he was with Bedini when he met President Franklin Pierce and the American Secretary of State, William L. Marcy. Bedini and Vertue also visited New York, Pittsburgh, Louisville, Baltimore, Philadelphia and New Orleans, before returning to Rome in January 1854. While in Rome, Vertue was himself made a monsignor (a *Cameriere d'Onore* to Pope Pius IX) in acknowledgement of his services. I imagine that it was not simply this ecclesiastical preferment that shaped his future, but also his wide travels and his meeting of senior politicians and Church leaders, which would come to be the hallmark of his ministry.

Bedini went on to senior curial appointments and was eventually appointed Cardinal in 1861. In 1854, Vertue returned to England and was for a brief six months in charge of the Catholic mission in Hackney. This was, at the time, in its infancy. The parish, or mission as it was called at the time, of St John the Baptist was founded in 1847, and a church opened in 1848 at the southern end of Mare Street (the present church was not built until 1956). Vertue's work would have been administering the sacraments and building up the community.

The Army Chaplains' Department was founded in September 1796, under the first Chaplain General, the Revd John Gamble, and finally given the "Royal" prefix in 1919 (hence RAChD). Initially only Church of England chaplains were recruited, but from 1827 Presbyterians were recognized, and Catholics were recruited from 1836. These days, all the chaplains are commissioned officers, but they do not carry standard officer ranks and are always addressed as Padre. Nevertheless, there are equivalent ranks and the chaplains wear their insignia on their uniforms. In the first instance, the chaplains' department was quite a small unit, but following the outbreak of the Crimean War in 1854, the chaplains' department grew, and given the dates, we can see that Vertue was most probably part of this expansion.

In the spring of 1855, Vertue was sent to Chatham (training) Camp in Kent, established by Royal Warrant in 1812, and on 24 June 1855 he was commissioned as a military chaplain, 4th class (equivalent to Captain). Today this base is the headquarters of the Royal School of Military Engineering (REME). Thereafter Vertue was posted to Aldershot for six years and he became the first Roman Catholic chaplain in the Army. It is worth noting that *commissioned* Roman Catholic chaplains to the army were only introduced on 1 April 1859, although existing Catholic chaplains had their seniority backdated.

The Catholic parish of Aldershot, now in the Diocese of Portsmouth, was not established until 1869, but in 1855, when Vertue arrived, a Catholic church dedicated to St Michael and St Sebastian was erected in the south camp. This large wooden and iron building, opposite the Louise Margaret Hospital, was not unlike a barn and served the needs of the Catholic population. Mgr Vertue was the first chaplain there.

Next, in 1861, Vertue's chaplaincy work took him to Bermuda, a British territory and military base some thousand miles east-southeast of Cape Hatteras in North Carolina. The island really is tiny, covering only 20.5 square miles, compared to (say) the Isle of Wight which has an area of some 150 square miles. The army barracks was established in 1701, primarily to defend the Royal Naval Dockyard, and to guard the coast. The Royal Engineers played a significant role here and were stationed at the St George's Garrison. The British Army base in Bermuda was finally closed in 1957.

During Vertue's time there, highly infectious yellow fever broke out on the island, and, as the only Catholic priest, he worked with outstanding courage and devotion. "It is recorded that on one occasion he was himself in bed with fever, but got up to administer viaticum to a dying member of his flock."[5] Of course, this implies that he had a much wider ministry, beyond his military duties. At the end of his term of service in Bermuda, he volunteered to stay on and continued to minister to the people. He was mentioned in the general orders of the Army, and he received a special vote of thanks from the War Office for his gallantry and conspicuous disregard of personal dangers.

In 1865, Vertue returned to England and served at Colchester. The army barracks there were established in 1794 and extended in 1800. From 1854–6, during the Crimean War, up to 5,000 troops were stationed there, and the base was again significant during the First World War. A significant Army presence remains in Colchester to this day.

Upon arrival, Vertue was initially promoted to chaplain, 3rd class (equivalent to Major) on 18 May, and then chaplain, 2nd class (equivalent to Lieutenant Colonel) on 2 February 1870. The 1871 census locates him in military accommodation at 114 Military Road, Colchester, living with his sister and his nephew, the future Fr Henry Kelly, then aged four. Also living with them were two servants, which suggests that Vertue was quite well paid, or at least well catered for by the Army. He lived next door to Edmund Albert Anderson and his wife, who is described as another "Chaplain to the Forces", most probably Church of England.

In 1871 (after the census), Vertue was sent to Portsmouth. Victoria, Cambridge and Clarence Barracks are all traditionally associated with Portsmouth, but Victoria was, in fact, not founded until 1886, as an overflow barracks to Clarence Barracks. In all likelihood, Vertue would have ministered to Catholics at both the other two. The Cambridge Barracks were established in 1825, converting some warehouse accommodation to military use. Between 1856 and 1859, these were extended, using red Flemish bricks and Welsh slate for the roofs, to provide officer accommodation. The barracks continued to be in use until the end of the First World War until the site was acquired by Portsmouth Grammar School in 1926.

The Clarence Barracks were established in 1760 and known originally as Fourhouse Barracks, built alongside an earlier Royal Marine Barracks between St Nicholas Road and the fortifications. The barracks were renamed the Clarence Barracks after a visit of the Duke of Clarence in 1827. In 1880, the barracks moved to a new site and a new building was built, reminiscent of a French chateau, using conscript labour from the prison. New officers' quarters and a parade ground were added in 1893. The buildings were eventually decommissioned and today house the Portsmouth Museum.

It was at Portsmouth that Vertue was again promoted to chaplain, 1st class (equivalent to Colonel), on 2 February 1875. He was one of about 15 to 20 chaplains, 1st class, and one of two Catholic chaplains, 1st class.

It was at this time that Vertue's life intersected with another notable Catholic, the Venerable Mother Mary Potter, foundress of the Little Company of Mary. Mary Potter was born on 22 November 1847, and in 1865, following the death of her father, she moved with her mother and her siblings from London to Southsea, in Portsmouth. Mary tried her vocation to the religious life with the Sisters of Mercy, but her poor health prevented her from pursuing this religious profession. She returned to Southsea and began to consider founding a religious community of her own.

Around 1872, Mary Potter joined a small group who attended confession and Mass at a private chapel in Ashburton Street, where Mgr Vertue lived. Vertue became Mary's spiritual director (and there is a series of extant letters from Mary to Mgr Vertue), but, by all accounts, he was not sympathetic to her plans for the new community. Mary Potter read St Grignon de Montfort's *Treatise on True Devotion to the Blessed Virgin*, translated by Fr Faber in 1862, and was profoundly influenced by it. But Vertue told her he disapproved of the *True Devotion*, saying it was almost condemned by the Church.[6] Mary Potter told Vertue about what she considered to be divine revelations, but Vertue admonished her and was convinced that she was delusional, and even neurotic.

In 1876, the spiritual relationship between Potter and Vertue ended, although we should note that Mary Potter eventually moved to Nottingham and founded the Little Company of Mary in 1877. She died in the Company's mother house in Rome in 1913 and was buried there. She was declared "Venerable", the first step towards canonization, by Pope St John Paul II in 1988 and her body was translated to the Cathedral of St Barnabas in Nottingham.

There is some speculation why Vertue failed to recognize the sanctity of Mary Potter. It was undoubtedly unusual for working-class women in the Victorian era to claim religious experiences and to propose new religious orders. There was perhaps also a wariness of women in general, and certainly Mary's convictions challenged the authority of Vertue, and the patriarchal position of the Church at the time, and in Victorian society more generally.

In 1878, Vertue went to Malta. The Pembroke Army Garrison was a collection of military installations around the town of Pembroke and Fort Pembroke, established in 1862. There was a significant army hospital there during the First World War and the base remained in use by the British until 1977, when it was handed over to the Maltese government. It is from Vertue's time in Malta that we have an extended description of him, courtesy of a Mr John Matthews and included in Vertue's obituary in *The Tablet*. He was a tall figure, with a rapid stride, reverent demeanour and clad in broadcloth, which was half ecclesiastical and half military. Vertue had keen grey eyes, behind gold-rimmed spectacles, which delivered a searching glance. The chapel in his house at Strada Vescovo had a little altar, with exquisite medieval paintings with which the prelate so much loved to surround himself.

Vertue celebrated the liturgy with great precision and order and had no toleration of careless or slipshod ways: his altar was always arranged with the most scrupulous exactness and his sacristy was a marvel of regularity and decorum. He himself was always properly dressed, and on formal occasions wore a long frock coat with colonel's crowns in gold braid on the collar and a broad stripe of black braid on the trouser! He was also sometimes seen in the full habit of an Italian priest, with buttoned cassock flowing, buckled shoes and a wide beaver hat. It is perhaps little surprise that he bore the nickname "John the Magnificent".

After his posting to Malta, Vertue left the military and was appointed the first Bishop of Portsmouth. At the time of his leaving, he appears in the Army List as the most senior (by date of appointment) of all the Army Chaplains, 1st class. It cannot be doubted that his evident success and promotion in the Army would have prepared him well for life leading a new diocese. Indeed, in announcing Vertue's appointment, *The Tablet* declared him to be a zealous priest and valued public servant, adding "his zeal and devotedness are well known and tested. During his labours for more than quarter of a century as Chaplain to the Forces, he has endeared himself not only to those in his spiritual charge, but to all with whom he has come in contact."[7]

On 19 May 1882, Pope Leo XIII issued an Apostolic Brief dividing the Diocese of Southwark, forming a new diocese out of the western part, to include Hampshire, Dorset, Berkshire, parts of south Oxfordshire, the Isle of Wight and the Channel Islands. Fr John Vertue was appointed as the first bishop (again by Pope Leo XIII) on 3 June, and he was consecrated by Cardinal Manning, assisted by Bishops Herbert Vaughan (then of Salford) and William Weathers (titular Bishop of Amycla), on 25 July 1882 in the Church of Our Lady of Victories, the pro-Cathedral in Kensington. On that very day, he sent his first pastoral letter, declaring that "what we seek is to enlarge the Kingdom of Christ".[8]

Very shortly afterwards, on the feast of St Lawrence (10 August), he took possession of the incomplete half-church in Portsmouth, where he was enthroned, and the church immediately became the diocesan cathedral. Bishop Coffin of Southwark, Bishop Hedley of Newport and most of the clergy of the new diocese were there. "Portsmouth" appeared for the first time in the "news from the dioceses" section of *The Tablet*, and it was reported that the new bishop took possession of his incomplete church, it having been blessed and Mass celebrated there for the first time, on the previous day by Fr John Horan, the former mission rector. Following the elaborate ceremonial, it was reported that a luncheon was afterwards provided.

The *Hampshire Telegraph* reported:

> Roman Catholicism in Portsmouth entered upon a fresh epoch in its history. Its dreary plodding struggles as a comparatively obscure mission ceased with that ceremony, and the responsible duties connected with the Episcopal See were formally undertaken. The faithful who have seen the welcome transition from the dark and dismal church with its equally gloomy approach in Prince George Street, to the stately interior of the new edifice, may consider themselves fortunate in their generation.[9]

Bishop Vertue petitioned the Holy See that the Blessed Virgin Mary and St Edmund of Abingdon be the patrons of the diocese (Abingdon lying within the new diocesan territory). Soon afterwards, Fr Horan was appointed as the first cathedral administrator. The chapter of the diocese was erected on 30 October (1882), and Dr John Crookhall was appointed first Provost and Canon John Baptist Cahill the first Pro-Vicar General. "Everything was very solemn and impressive, and worthy of the great and important occasion."[10] The bishop gave his solemn blessing and published an indulgence of 40 days. Two years later, in (July) 1884, the first diocesan synod was convoked, which every priest was bound to attend. These were annual events until they were discontinued by Bishop Cahill.

As well as getting his new diocese up and running, Vertue found time to confirm 76 persons (adults and children) in St Joseph's Church, Southampton on 13 August 1882. On 15 September, he arrived in Jersey for a High Mass and confirmation, and he then travelled on to Guernsey (20 September) and Alderney too, where he confirmed 12 children. In October, he issued another pastoral letter to mark "Rosary Sunday" (7 October is the feast of Our Lady of the Rosary, instituted by Pope St Pius V).

The cathedral was completed in the years that followed, and much of the money needed for completion came from the poorer members of the community, hence the sobriquet "The Penny Brick Church". The cathedral and its altar were consecrated by Bishop Vertue on 29 March 1887, and the *Portsmouth Evening News* commented on the "elaborate ritual . . . characterized by an unusual gorgeousness of pomp and circumstance".

While Vertue was bishop, 18 new churches were built, two orphanages and a number of schools. In particular, we may note the opening of the first Catholic church in Shanklin (on the Isle of Wight) on 21 July 1888. At the High Mass, the bishop explained that he had received a request for a regular Mass in the town. He visited with his vicar general, Mgr Cahill, and saw a suitable site in Atherley Road which he committed to buying, and Sir Philip Rose had offered to build the church. At the opening Mass, Mgr Cahill was the celebrant, assisted by Fr Ellard as deacon and Fr George Dolman as sub-deacon. This original tin church was replaced by a Flemish Gothic brick church in 1907, which was in turn bombed in the Second World War and destroyed on 3 January 1943. Several members of the Shanklin congregation lost their lives and were buried in the ruins.

The Catholic mission at Petersfield was revived in 1890. The Cave family had established their home at Ditcham Park in 1885, where they had a public chapel served by their own chaplain. In 1890, Lawrence Trent Cave bought land in Station Road for a Catholic church to be built, and commissioned a design by John Kelly, who also notably designed St Patrick's, Soho Square. The church is a cruciform design, in an Italian style with nave, transepts and two side chapels. It has an octagonal copper dome surmounted by a lantern. The altar and the font are marble. An apse and transepts were added later. Bishop Vertue opened the church in 1891, although it was not consecrated until 1933.

Catholic provision in Lyndhurst was originally a monthly Mass celebrated in a small building in Wellands Road, the alternative being a ten-mile journey to Lymington. In 1895, the church of the Assumption of Our Lady and St Edward the Confessor in Lyndhurst was erected and paid for in full by Edouard Souberbielle, a doctor of the French Court, as a memorial to his wife Marie Louise, who died on 14 May 1894 whilst holidaying in the New Forest. The architect was Sir Reginald Blomfield, principal architect of the War Graves Commission.

In the Early English style, the church is a Grade II listed building of stone with Bath stone mouldings. On the north outside wall, there is a fine buttress with an ornate capping and a small statue of Our Lady with the infant Jesus. There is a spire surmounted by a golden cockerel. Paintings, statues and fine stained glass adorn the interior. As the total cost of some £5,000 was all paid by M. Souberbielle, it was possible to consecrate the church as soon as it was finished, and this was done by Bishop Vertue, assisted by the parish priest, Canon James Daly, and the parish priest of Lymington, Fr Patrick O'Connell, on 28 July 1896, from 8 a.m. until 12 noon. The bishop returned in July 1897 to confirm the first seven confirmation candidates.

After a period of occasional Masses only, the Jesuits moved to Bournemouth in 1869 and opened a small chapel. In 1870, a temporary wooden chapel was built and a new church dedicated to the Sacred Heart was first opened in 1873 and completed in 1875. As the town of Bournemouth expanded a Catholic community grew in Boscombe and the church of Corpus Christi there was founded by Baroness Pauline von Hügel in 1895. A church was begun which was opened by Bishop

Vertue on 8 September 1896, and Boscombe was established as a distinct parish in 1897.

But we should not think of Bishop Vertue as an ecclesiastical administrator only, although he undoubtedly had gifts when it came to ruling and guiding, based on a very organized approach to life. He was a scholarly man too: a Fellow of the Society of Antiquarians, a member of the Archaeological Institute, and Vice President of the Hampshire Record Society. He published a prayer book for Army use, and a revised version of Challoner's *Meditations* (first published in 1753). Finally, Bishop Vertue was also noted for the care and devotedness he extended to his charges, perhaps most notably during the yellow fever outbreak in Bermuda. He would be remembered as a gentleman with an unwavering sense of duty.

Vertue was a traveller too. He made a number of trips to Rome: in 1883 as a newly ordained bishop when he stayed at the Venerable English College and was received by Pope Leo XIII; again from December 1887—January 1888, when he participated in Pope Leo's jubilee festivities, and finally in 1896. Moreover, and rather unusually for the times, he travelled to the United States in 1889, following Pope Leo XIII's promulgation of his encyclical *Magni nobis* to celebrate the centenary of the establishment of the American Catholic hierarchy. There were many celebrations, especially in Baltimore and Washington (at the newly established Catholic University of America), and Bishop Vertue represented the English bishops at these events.

Bishop Vertue died (aged 74) on Wednesday 23 May 1900, the eve of Ascension Day, in Bishop's House, Portsmouth. He had been ill for some time (and indeed said his last Mass on Easter Day) with what was described as blood poisoning, perhaps septicaemia, and his death was not unexpected. At his bedside at the end were his "sister Mrs. Kelly, and his niece Miss Kelly; Bishop Cahill, Dr Driver, Fathers Tremble, Cotter, Haythornthwaite and Russell and Mr Collins".[11]

The body of the bishop in full pontificals and encased in an oak coffin lay in state in the great hall where it was visited by many people. It was borne to the cathedral on Monday (28 May) and placed on a catafalque bearing the episcopal coat of arms and surrounded by a number of unclarified wax candles. The bishop's mitre and mozetta were placed on top of the coffin that bore the inscription '*Johannes Vertue, primus Portus Magni episcopus. Obit xxiii Maii MCM*' (We may note in passing here that the Latin name of the diocese was changed by the Sacred Congregation *Propaganda Fide*, from *Portsmuthensis* to *Portus Magnus* in September 1888.) At 3 p.m., vespers for the dead was chanted, led by the bishop of Thagora (that is Bishop Cahill), and at 6.30 p.m., the solemn dirge was sung.

On Tuesday, the Requiem Mass was offered by Bishop Cahill with some 60 other priests in attendance, including Canon Gumming who was the deacon and Canon Collins who was the subdeacon. Following the Mass, the five absolutions were sung, unaccompanied, which was said to be most impressive. After the service, the coffin was taken in procession to Highland Park Cemetery as the 129th and 50th (*Miserere*) psalms were sung. Bishop Cahill blessed the grave and solemnly buried Bishop Vertue.

The private mourners were Mrs Frances Anne Kelly (née Vertue), the late bishop's sister, who was born in 1828 and was the wife of John Kelly. She attended with four of her (nine or) ten children, including Father Henry Leo Paul Kelly, nephew of the late bishop. Father Henry was born in 1866, also studied at the Venerable English College in Rome, was ordained in 1891, and died in 1944 near Lymington in Hampshire.

Bishop Cahill executed Bishop Vertue's will and estate of £100 19s 6d. In addition, the bishop, who was noted as a great bibliophile, left a collection of rare and interesting works, some of which, particularly the *incunabula*—books printed before 1500—went to the college library at Stonyhurst.

The memory of Bishop Vertue was "of a strong, kind man, a strict and conscientious officer, a prelate cultured and refined, a priest who lived in the presence of his God. May his soul rest in that presence forever!"[12] A committee was convened to choose how Bishop Vertue should be best commemorated, and a memorial cross was erected over his tomb costing about £120. There were also some additional funds which were used to decorate and complete the Lady Chapel in the cathedral.

Notes

1   *The Tablet*, 26 May 1900, p. 820.

2   *The Catholic Directory and Annual Register* 1840, vols 3–4, p. 84.

3   Anthony Kenny, *A Path from Rome* (London: Sidgwick & Jackson, 1985), p. 53.

4   Gerard Dwyer, *Diocese of Portsmouth: Past and Present* (Portsmouth: Portsmouth Diocesan Centenary Committee, 1981), p. 61.

5   Ibid.

6   Cf. Elizabeth Gilroy, *Mary Potter* (London: CTS, 2010), p. 27.

7   *The Tablet*, 29 July 1882, p. 160.

8   Letter quoted in full in *The Tablet*, 12 August 1882, p. 273.

9   *Hampshire Telegraph*, 12 August 1882, p. 5.

10   *The Tablet*, 4 November 1882, p. 754.

11   *The Tablet*, 26 May 1900, p. 829.

12   Ibid., p. 821.

2

John Baptist Cahill (1900–10)

John Baptist Cahill was born on 2 September 1841. According to records in the Portsmouth diocesan archive, his parents were Thomas and Joanna Cahill from Ireland, and it is recorded that he was born in London, the youngest of three boys. Records of foundation Masses, established by Cahill himself, confirm his mother was Joanna (*d*.4 August, year unknown) and his father was Thomas (*d*.30 May). The 1851 census records a John Cahill living with his parents, J. Cahill and A. Cahill, at 7 Drake Street, in the (Church of England) parish of St George the Martyr, Holborn, which seems the closest fit of all the census records that there are, but the match is not exact. I can find no record of Cahill's baptism or early schooling, and so his young years remain something of a mystery. As an aside, we may note that in the 1851 census Cahill's elder brother Edward (*b*.1835), and the middle of the three, is listed as a resident student at St Edmund's College, Ware, to which in due course Cahill himself would proceed. Cahill's eldest brother was Thomas (*b*.1822).

The 1861 census gives quite a detailed entry for "The Old Hall Green, St Edmund's College (Ware) in the Parish of Standon (and the registration district of Standon), Hertfordshire". At that time, there were nine clerical professors under the principal Fr William Weathers, and a lay professor of French. There were a further five clergy recorded as students—presumably ordained deacons in their final year. The remainder of the student body consisted of 29 scholars and 42 students, all assisted by nine servants, seven of whom were women detailed to cook, wash, clean and manage the domestic side of college life.

In 1854, when young Cahill, aged 13, arrived, the school-cum-seminary was in the ascendant. His obituary in *The Edmundian* speaks of the particularly high quality of music at the school at the time, under the Revd James Landers. Cahill is praised for his singing. There is talk of Mozart and Haydn, presumably Masses and motets, and it is said of Cahill, that music was "his chief accomplishment",[1] albeit not his only one, for he showed great talent. No other records, for example school reports, seem to have survived.

Cahill probably finished his schooling in 1859, but whilst still residing in the college (the "seminary department" one presumes), he matriculated at London University. The census for 1861 has him as a student resident at The Old Hall Green, St Edmund's College. He went on to graduate with a London B.A. degree in 1862,[2] although the *Edmundian* obituary suggests that this was a B.D. degree, and if Cahill was an "external candidate", this is perhaps more likely. Either way, following graduation with a bachelor's degree, he would have concluded his preparations for ordination. It is recorded that he was a member of the teaching staff (a "professor") at the college from 1863 to 1864. At the end of this academic year, his school and college days were complete and he was ordained to the priesthood.

Cahill was ordained priest in Bermondsey by Bishop Grant (of Southwark) on 16 October 1864. Some sources put his ordination date as 4 October, but, in a note in the diocesan archive, Cahill himself writes that this is a common error and that his ordination was 16 October. He was sent to the old St John's Church in Prince George Street, Southsea, to assist Fr Henry Philips.

A short time later, in June 1866, Fr Philips went to St Mary's, Ryde on the Isle of Wight to be parish priest or rector, and Cahill was sent with him to be his curate. Philips was the successor of Fr John Telford, a devoted and indefatigable man who served at Ryde for some 19 years (1846–65) and who was praised by bishop and people alike at his requiem. By contrast, Philips from Portsea was a man of poor health, indeed he had previously held the senior position of Dean of Hampshire and the Isle of Wight, but following a decline in his health in Portsea, had been transferred to Ryde for a quieter life. No doubt then that his energy and enthusiasm were in decline. Further, Philips was in the unenviable position of having Elizabeth Countess of Clare in his congregation. She was a forceful woman of means who had financed the building of St Mary's just 20 years earlier (building began in 1844 and the church opened in 1846). No doubt she still exercised certain proprietary claims, and indeed she had her own private chapel above the sacristy, which still exists to this day. Additionally, he must have struggled to form a relationship with the countess that was anything like that of his longstanding predecessor.

So it was a shrewd move on the part of Bishop Grant to send the young Cahill to Ryde too as curate. According to Clarke, "Cahill impressed the Countess with his manners, correctness and his love of the Gothic style in architecture and worship" and furthermore "parishioners warmed to him quickly".[3] At this time, with Queen Victoria regularly visiting Osborne House, the Isle of Wight was rapidly becoming a fashionable place to be, and Cahill would have been kept busy as a curate. As well as the normal round of liturgical functions "at home", he regularly went to Shanklin to hear confessions and say Mass. It is thought that it was around this time that Cahill first met the Jesuit priest and poet Gerard Manley Hopkins, who described the south coast of the Isle of Wight as "luxuriant vegetation with wild and gentle scenery. The sea is brilliantly coloured and always calm and the bathing is delightful."[4] It should be noted that other literary figures such as Keats, Longfellow and Dickens were also visitors to the island around that time.

In 1868, Fr Philips resigned as Rector of Ryde on grounds of ill health, and despite his youth, and perhaps upon the recommendation of the Countess of Clare, Bishop Grant appointed Cahill as the Rector of Ryde, a post he would occupy for the next 32 years. In the death notice carried in the *Isle of Wight Observer*, dated 11 August 1910, Cahill is described as "having an attractive personality and a genial and kindly nature". His services were popular, "owing chiefly to the beautiful singing and to his eloquent preaching", and he himself was the "possessor of a fine base [sic] voice".[5] The following week in the funeral notice, the newspaper referred to the affection and esteem in which he was held, and acknowledged his "genial kindness to all of whom he was brought in contact [sic], and his unobtrusive charity to all who needed it".[6] So it seems he was a highly regarded and popular man, and as we shall see later the numbers who turned out at his funeral were large, a genuine tribute to an extraordinary priest and bishop.

Before we turn to some of the remarkable and extraordinary things that he did, it is worth considering for a moment the ordinary life of a priest in the late nineteenth century. At the heart of his life would have been a daily Mass. Concelebration did not occur at that time, and even if there was no public Mass, a priest would have said Mass with a sole server. This would have taken the best part of an hour. Anthony Kenny reminds us that (before the Second Vatican Council) ordination to the subdiaconate obliged one to recite the daily office:

> Matins, Lauds, Prime, Terce, Sext, None, Vespers and Compline: services which in a monastery would be sung in church at the appropriate hour from Matins in the early hours of the morning to Compline at bedtime. A diocesan priest or seminarist instead of singing these services publicly recites them in solitary silence (although one's lips and tongue must move or one's obligation remains unfulfilled). The recitation of the office took about an hour a day.[7]

In addition to these, Cahill would have had other public services to lead: baptisms, marriages and funerals, not to mention devotions which were much more popular in Victorian times than they are today. For example, records show that in 1874 the "Children of Mary" and the "Confraternity of the Blessed Sacrament" were established, and these would have been involved in "leading processions, cleaning the church, arranging flowers and always present for devotions and novenas".[8] In addition to this, there would have been a range of pastoral tasks, visits and the like, and so we can well imagine that the priest's life was certainly a busy one. However, Cahill somehow found time to achieve a whole range of other things as well.

Most significantly, he maintained a close relationship with Elizabeth Countess of Clare, who as mentioned earlier funded the building of St Mary's Church. Following her husband's death in 1851, the countess threw herself into many philanthropic projects which she would have no doubt discussed at length with Fr Telford, Fr Philips and later Cahill. In his biography of her, Peter Clarke suggests Cahill and the countess got on very well, but that this was on account of Cahill's deference and diplomacy. The remark that Fr Cahill would often consult the countess over the choice of music is particularly telling! Additionally, there is evidence that Cahill shared and encouraged the countess' devotion to the Blessed Virgin Mary. Such devotions were on the increase generally following the declaration of the Dogma of the Immaculate Conception in 1854 and the apparitions in Lourdes in 1858. The outdoor processions in Ryde, in honour of Our Lady, which began in 1869 are evidence of this.

Additionally, we may note the countess' interest in, and affection for, the Dominican order (which she herself considered joining). Indeed, one of her most notable achievements was the establishment, and ongoing support, of the Dominican Priory at Carisbrooke. The foundation stone for the building, the first new monastic institution since the Reformation, was laid in 1865, and the first nuns arrived sometime thereafter. It is unthinkable that Cahill would not have been quite seriously involved with this project and also with the unprecedented visit of Queen Victoria to the priory in 1869.

Further evidence of Cahill's tact can be inferred since it is almost certainly no coincidence that the building works and alterations that Cahill made to St Mary's Church began the year after the countess died in 1879. Perhaps some of these plans were hatched together, but more likely, it seems to me, is that Cahill had to bide his time until he could exercise a completely free hand.

Firstly, in 1880 he added a rose window in the sanctuary by Nathaniel Westlake F.S.A. as a memorial to the countess. Secondly, in 1882 he added a porch in the northwest corner with notable stained glass: a lancet window depicting the seven sacraments of the Church in memory of his two priest-brothers. Thirdly, following a request of Pope Leo XIII, that England should rededicate itself to the patronage of Mary, a Lady Chapel was added in 1893. The design of the chapel was by Cahill's friend Canon A. J. Scholes and the altar (one of the first to depict Our Lady of Walsingham) was by Pugin. Much of the work was funded by a parishioner: Frederic de Courcy-May. The chapel was blessed by Bishop Vertue, assisted by Cahill. In 1894, Cahill commissioned Westlake (again) to paint some of the mysteries of the rosary and other biblical scenes which adorn the ceiling and the walls. These fine paintings were restored by Marianne Rodrigues in 1993. The stained glass in the chapel is notable too. Fourthly and finally, a Sacred Heart chapel, again designed by Scholes and consecrated by Bishop Vertue in March 1898, was added in the northeast corner, made memorable by the effective use of translucent alabaster and marble.

So we can see that Cahill was a busy and enterprising man when it came to building work. He was not nervous or backward about undertaking fairly major projects and he had the ability to raise the necessary funds too.

In addition to her philanthropic work, the countess was also a woman of vision who once declared that she wanted the children of Ryde to experience the joy of a Catholic education. The first "schooling" took place in the church crypt, but in the mid-1850s a school was built on the edge of the church property and in 1856 it is recorded that the school had 21 boys and 20 girls taught in separate classes. Later, Cahill was a regular visitor to the school, and it appears that religious instruction was very much at the heart of school life. Following the death of the countess, and probably in the early 1880s, Cahill approached the Sisters of the Convent of Mercy in Abingdon and invited them to establish a new convent and boarding school at Ryde. In October 1884 the new nuns arrived.

As if all this were not enough, Cahill also found himself sharing his presbytery with, and no doubt looking after, a variety of visitors, including both of his brothers who liked to visit. But these were not only social visits; it seems Cahill had to be something of a carer too. Cahill's elder brother Thomas (a priest of the Diocese of Westminster) made his final visit to Ryde in 1876. He died on 31 January at the young (even by Victorian standards) age of 44 and was buried in Ryde cemetery.

A similar thing happened again in 1889. Cahill's brother Edward (a priest of the Diocese of Southwark), who had formerly served at St George's Cathedral, had been "an invalid for some three years"[9] and had presumably been cared for by Cahill at the last. He died aged 54, on 2 July 1889, and Canon Doyle presided over the liturgies in the absence of Bishop Vertue. Following an overnight rest in St Mary's Church, a requiem was celebrated, and the body was then taken to Ryde cemetery and buried alongside his brother. However strong Cahill's own faith, the death and burial of a second brother, and a brother priest, cannot have failed to take its toll.

Perhaps most remarkable of all was the visit of Bishop Vertue himself. Recall that the Diocese of Portsmouth was created in May 1882; Mgr John Vertue was appointed the first bishop and consecrated in July 1882. But his cathedral was still under construction, and he certainly did not have a clergy house, let alone a bishop's palace, to live in. He records in his diary "*deficiente residentia propria*",[10] and he went to live in St Mary's Ryde until 29 March 1884, when the episcopal residence was complete.

Additionally, and most unusually, the first ordination to the priesthood in the new diocese took place, not in the cathedral in Portsmouth, but in St Mary's Church in Ryde. It is said that a Fr Rivara, put in charge of the new mission in Southampton, claimed in a speech to be the first to be ordained in the new diocese, but there is no mention of him in the records. The first recorded ordination is that of Pierce William Greene. Vertue wrote "on the feast of the Apostles Peter and Paul, in the church of St Mary, Ryde, 29 June 1883, dimissorial letters having been received from the Bishop of Cloyne, we ordained to the priesthood, Pierce William Greene".[11]

We can imagine that Cahill enjoyed having his bishop living with him, but it cannot have always been a blessing and no doubt it entailed extra work for Cahill, who must have had to make time to listen to and advise his boss on the governance and development of the new diocese, if nothing else. It would seem that he made a great job of it, however, and he obviously won the respect and the affection of his bishop and no doubt as a result was quickly promoted within the diocese. In August 1882, Vertue appointed Cahill Pro-Vicar General, confirming the post the following year. In 1883, Cahill was appointed as Privy Chamberlain to Pope Leo XIII, and in 1887, he was appointed as a Domestic Prelate (i.e. a Monsignor). In 1888, he was appointed as Provost, i.e. head of the cathedral chapter. In 1892, he was appointed Protonotary Apostolic, and it was at this time that Fr William Timothy Cotter was appointed as his curate.

As we shall see, Cahill's secretary William Cotter was an Irishman, born in Cork in 1866, who studied at St Colman's College, Fermoy, County Cork and prepared for the priesthood at Maynooth College, County Kildare. Following his ordination in 1892, he was sent to England and to Portsmouth on the missions. When Cahill was raised to the purple, Cotter succeeded him as Rector of Ryde and became his secretary. Not long after, he (Cotter) was promoted to Canon, and in 1905 as auxiliary bishop in the diocese (see below). On Cahill's death it was his old friend, secretary and successor in Ryde who succeeded him as the third Bishop of Portsmouth.

It seems that Cahill made a number of trips to Rome with Bishop Vertue. The bishop's diary records a first visit with Cahill, departing on 9 April 1883 and staying at the Venerable English College while they were there. Vertue records that they were received by Pope Leo XIII on 5 May. A second visit was made, departing 19 December 1887, and Vertue and Cahill stayed in Rome until 27 January 1888, participating in the jubilee festivities of Pope Leo. Vertue made a third trip to Rome in April 1896, but Cahill is not recorded as accompanying him on this occasion.

It seems entirely fitting then, that after a long, distinguished and successful ministry Cahill was honoured with the rank of bishop, although he himself said he became a bishop too late in life! He was consecrated titular bishop of Thagora in Portsmouth Cathedral on 1 May 1900, by Bishop (later Cardinal) Francis Bourne, Archbishop of Westminster, assisted by Bishop John Hadley from the Diocese of Newport and Menevia and Bishop Charles Graham, titular of Cisamus and auxiliary bishop of Plymouth. He took as his episcopal motto *in Domino confido*, "I trust in the Lord". Cahill's friends in Ryde presented him with an episcopal ring, a large emerald surrounded with diamonds, and other friends gave him a pectoral cross and chain. It was barely weeks later that Bishop Vertue became ill and died. The newly consecrated Bishop Cahill was at his side when he died. He was the sole executor of Vertue's will, and in due course he succeeded him as Bishop of Portsmouth, an appointment that was confirmed on 25 August of that year, 1900.

The first remarkable thing about Bishop Cahill's time as bishop is that, for three years at least, he continued to live in Ryde. No doubt he was profoundly attached to the place after many years and much valued the proximity of his secretary, Fr Cotter. According to his diary entry on 20 September 1903, he "assisted in the procession for the opening of the 40 hours devotion at Ryde, which I am now leaving for Portsmouth after uninterrupted residence of 37 years",[12] confirming Cahill's arrival in Ryde (as curate) in 1866.

Perhaps the most important part of Cahill's episcopal ministry is that he continued the work of strengthening and building the diocese, begun by his predecessor. When Portsmouth Diocese separated from

Southwark, there were 55 chapels in 40 missions (parishes) and 49 priests. In 1901, when Cahill took over the diocese, there were 77 churches and chapels in 50 separate missionary districts and 62 diocesan priests; and it is recorded that during his episcopacy 13 new missions or parishes were opened; amongst them Basingstoke; St Swithun's Southsea; Holy Cross, Eastleigh; St Joseph's at Copnor, and the tiny chapel of the Assumption at Gorey Village in Jersey, which was opened in 1903, to name but a few. In 1906, Cahill turned his attention to the cathedral and completed the building by adding narthex, porch and turrets designed by the priest-architect Canon Alexander Scholes, who had worked so closely on a number of projects in Ryde and was obviously highly regarded by Cahill. At the same time, the high altar and baldacchino were raised and brought forward into the chancel in front of the screen.

But it was not only with diocesan churches that Cahill concerned himself. In 1901, the French government passed a law forbidding "religious association" without a suitable permit, and in 1902 parliament rejected *en bloc* all requests for such permits, effectively banning all religious from France! Cahill welcomed the fugitive monks and nuns, religious brothers and sisters into his diocese. This was a great gesture of fraternity and solidarity, motivated, no doubt, by Cahill's generosity of spirit, but it also did much to strengthen Catholic life in the diocese.

Some of the Benedictine monks from Solesmes founded a house at Farnborough in Hampshire in 1896. The original church had been built by Empress Eugenie to be a mausoleum for her husband Napoleon III. The church was opened by Bishop Vertue in 1887. With the arrival of the French monks, under Abbott Cabrol who was elected in 1903, the abbey and church expanded and became a centre of study and liturgical excellence. The new abbey church was consecrated by Bishop Cotter, Cahill's auxiliary, in 1908.

The Benedictine community (and school) of St Edmund from Douai was expelled in 1903, but they were welcomed by Cahill who invited them to settle in Woolhampton, taking over the parish and school of St Mary there. Cahill wrote in his diary on 22 July 1903: "Have today handed over St Mary's College Woolhampton to the English Benedictines exiled from Douai."[13] The new monks struggled at first, but in 1909 the decision was made to remain at Woolhampton and the property was bought by the monks from the bishop. The Holy See itself decreed that the historic name of Douai should be retained. The notable new abbey church was begun in 1928 and completed in 1933.

It was not only monks; Benedictine nuns also came to the Isle of Wight from St Cecilia's Abbey in Solesmes in 1901 following the passing of the new French association laws. At first, they settled in Northwood House, but they subsequently acquired, and moved to, Appley House in Ryde which they adapted to meet their religious needs. In 1921, the Appley nuns returned to Solesmes, and in 1922 the Benedictine Community of *Pax Cordis Jesu* at Ventnor (founded 1882) moved to the vacated priory. It became an abbey in 1926.

Additionally, from France, the Salesian Fathers opened a house in Guernsey in 1903, and the de la Salle Brothers opened two houses in Guernsey in 1904. There was also a community of Jesuits in Jersey, involved in schooling and formation, including the famous priest Teilhard de Chardin.

Perhaps closest to Bishop Cahill's heart were the Benedictine monks from Solesmes who recognized the rapidly deteriorating political situation in France and moved to the Isle of Wight in 1901. At first, they settled in Appuldurcombe House near Wroxall, and when it became clear that their exile would be more than temporary, they built a timber and corrugated iron church there. However, the monks' lease was to expire in 1908 and so, with encouragement from Cahill, they bought Quarr Abbey House on 24 May 1907. Situated on the north coast of the island this was the site of the ruins of a medieval Cistercian house which had been suppressed under King Henry VIII in 1537. The monk and architect Dom Paul Bellot began building (assisted by local workmen) with red bricks imported from Belgium. By 1908, the first phase of the monastic building was complete, and in 1911 work on the abbey church began. The church was completed the following year and consecrated on 12 October 1912.

It is worth noting that in the early 1880s Cahill instituted an annual parish walk from Ryde to the Cistercian ruins to pray for the return of monks to Quarr. It must have been a cause of great happiness to Cahill when this prayer was answered. It is recorded that Cahill enjoyed a close friendship with Abbott Delatte, and it is notable that during his time as bishop he celebrated the annual Chrism Mass not in the cathedral but at Appuldurcombe. This may seem odd to us because these days the bishop usually celebrates the Chrism Mass on Tuesday, Wednesday or Thursday of Holy Week, in the cathedral, with all his priests around him, who celebrate and recommit themselves to ministerial priesthood. But Greenacre and Haselock remind us that it was not always so; indeed, before the liturgical reforms of Pope Paul VI, the *Missa Chrismatis* was solely for the purpose of consecrating the holy oils for baptism, confirmation, ordination and the anointing of the sick.[14] In other words, there was no element of "priestly renewal" in the pre-conciliar Chrism Mass, so perhaps it should not surprise us overly that Cahill celebrated it at Appuldurcombe.

Bishop Cahill was also something of a letter writer. In the Southwark Diocese, Bishop Grant had decreed that a collection was to be taken each Rosary Sunday for the work of the diocese. When Portsmouth separated from Southwark, this collection on Rosary Sunday continued, and Bishop Cahill wrote to the parishes each year telling them of the financial needs and wants of the diocese and how the monies were spent.

Firstly, the bishop observed that whilst some parishes were financially self-sufficient others needed support, via allowances, totalling £670 in 1900. Additionally, there were historic debts associated with the building of new churches that the diocese needed to repay. Cahill was also keen for there to be a contingency fund for exceptional cases, and additionally there were new projects to be undertaken, specifically a school in Cowes and a boys' orphanage.

But the letters were not all about financial matters, and during Advent 1901, Cahill wrote to all the parishes appealing for vocations to the priesthood. Specifically he encouraged parents to foster vocations among their sons. He was anxious that of the 62 secular priests working in the diocese, only 37 were born in England, and of the remainder no less than 13 were on loan to the diocese and did not formally belong to it. It is difficult to assess exactly how successful his appeal was, but there was a definite increase in the number of diocesan priests while Cahill was bishop, and if nothing else, this letter clearly indicates a bishop who was not resting on his laurels but was actively building and developing his diocese.

Finally, on a lighter note—for us I mean, not for Cahill—in 1909, the bishop sent a circular to his clergy concerning the use of bicycles. Whilst the use of bicycles was permitted and indeed encouraged, the clergy were told that there was to be no associated relaxation of clerical dress, although a slight shortening of the clerical coat would be permitted, if necessary. Cahill reminded his clergy that their dress marked them out as ministers of God, and "the putting off of the clerical dress in order to mix with greater freedom in lay society is absolutely forbidden".[15]

I referred above to Cahill's visits to Rome with Bishop Vertue, but we may note that he made two further trips to Rome as bishop: the first in early May 1904, and again in October 1908, where along with a number of other English bishops he joined the extended jubilee celebrations for the fiftieth anniversary of the priestly ordination of Pope (now Saint) Pius X. Notices in *The Tablet* and letters in the Southwark diocesan archive refer to these visits, and on the second of these trips (when there was a huge number of visitors in Rome) Cahill spent part of his time, at least, in the Hotel d'Angleterre in Via Bocca di Leone in Rome. Today it is described as an iconic hotel preferred by the international jet set. I suspect it was rather more refined in Bishop Cahill's day!

Towards the end of his life, Cahill's health began to fail. On 2 October 1904, he fell seriously ill and indeed all hope of his recovery had been given up. The last rites, as they were then called, were administered. He subsequently wrote:

> On Sunday night, 11 December, I was at my worst. On Monday 12 December the recovery had begun; and on the Octave day of the feast, the physician announced to my household that my recovery was now assured . . . It was the gift of God, granted by our Blessed Mother during her Octave. Its sudden and permanent character justifies the word miraculous.[16]

But however miraculous and permanent, Cahill had already applied to Rome to be granted an auxiliary (helper) bishop, which was an unusual step at that time. Pope Pius X agreed to Cahill's request and Cahill's secretary William Cotter was duly appointed. On 19 March, he was consecrated titular bishop of *Clazomenae* and auxiliary bishop of Portsmouth by Cahill, assisted by the Bishops of Clifton and Southwark. The Bishop of Cloyne was also invited and the Abbott of Solesmes, said to be desirous of giving a token of his affection, also sent 20–25 monks to form the *schola*. Later, when Cotter succeeded Cahill as diocesan bishop, he took the motto *non recuso laborem* ("I will not refuse work"). Fr John Henry King became Cahill's new private secretary.

Cahill publicly declared his gratitude to the Holy Father for giving him an auxiliary, and he continued his work, but his health continued to deteriorate. In 1907, Cahill petitioned the Holy See to be allowed to change the annual clergy synod, begun by Bishop Vertue in 1884, to a triennial one, and the Pope granted him the right to use his discretion concerning such matters. As it happens, the Code of Canon Law promulgated in 1917 did away with the requirement for an annual diocesan clergy synod altogether. Although it is difficult to judge, I think this probably indicates quite a high degree of cordiality, even friendship between Cahill and Pope Pius.

Eventually, ill heath got the better of the hardworking Cahill, and he died on Tuesday 2 August 1910, a few weeks shy of his sixty-ninth birthday. The ceremonies following his death were elaborate, and indeed indicated the respect in which he was held. By Sunday 7 August, his remains had been placed in a leaden coffin, with an outer shell of polished oak which was carried from Bishop's House to the cathedral and placed on trestles draped in purple. According to the *Isle of Wight Observer*, there was a huge crowd at the Sunday evening service in the cathedral. Vespers of the day were sung, followed by benediction, the singing of Allegri's setting of *Miserere*, and then vespers of the dead, and so we can imagine a great and solemn occasion. Mr Fritz Wiber, formerly of Ryde, played Chopin's Funeral March on the grand organ to conclude proceedings.

On Monday, the coffin lay in state, many nuns of the diocese kept watch and a long procession of many clergy, secular and religious came to pay their last respects. Among them was the Archbishop of Westminster, Cardinal Francis Bourne, who gave his absolution at the conclusion of the singing of a solemn dirge. The following day, Tuesday (at 10.30 a.m.), the archbishop celebrated Cahill's requiem, and the sanctuary was crowded with bishops and abbots. Cahill's obituary in *The Tablet*[17] asserts that there were nearly 100 priests present—surely a mark of the affection and respect in which he was held—and the naval Commander-in-Chief of Portsmouth was also there. Following the funeral, Cahill's coffin was taken in solemn procession to Clarence Pier and then placed amidships on the upper deck of a special steamer and ferried to Ryde with all the attendant dignitaries, both ecclesiastical and civic. During the journey, hymns were sung and the rosary recited.

The *Isle of Wight Observer* of 6 August suggests that the coffin would then be met by a special train taking it to Ryde Esplanade Station and there placed in an open car for the final journey to Ryde Cemetery, accompanied by carriages for the most senior dignitaries and the remainder on foot. The bishop's mitre rested on the coffin, and the streets along the way were lined with reverent onlookers and mourners, most of the shops being closed. The bishops pronounced the final prayers of committal at the graveside amid a "vast concourse of people whose respectful behaviour was in keeping with the sad occasion".[18] The inscription on the plate of his coffin was "John Baptist Cahill, Second Bishop of Portsmouth, Born 2 September 1841, Died 2 August 1910, *Confidit in Domino. Animae ejus proprietur Deus!*"

Cahill's auxiliary William Timothy Cotter succeeded Cahill and remained as Bishop of Portsmouth from 1910–40. In 1912, he erected the Stations of the Cross in the cathedral as a permanent memorial to Bishop Cahill.

The epitaph on Cahill's coffin was an eminently fitting one. It seems that "he trusted in the Lord and his soul belonged to God" accurately captures and summarizes the whole of Cahill's life. From an early age, he followed his older brothers to the seminary; he excelled there and proceeded to priestly ordination. Despite the many attractions that Ryde undoubtedly has, it is remarkable that Cahill stayed there for so long. He was undoubtedly a shrewd, capable and holy man and other possibilities must have beckoned, but he stayed faithful to serving the parish of St Mary's. His soul was content in God. On a more human level, I think Cahill's stability and contentment must have been, in part, on account of the close bonds of affection that he formed with Bishop Vertue who preceded him in Portsmouth and Fr Thomas Cotter who succeeded him. Indeed, the tone of many of the letters between Cahill and Vertue stored in the Portsmouth diocesan archive points to a close and affectionate relationship between the two. It was surely not only on account of his office that Cahill executed Vertue's will and presided at his funeral.

As bishop himself, Cahill worked tirelessly; despite his own declining health, he trusted in the Lord and built up the diocese. He enlarged the cathedral, increased the number of churches and priests in the diocese and welcomed many French religious fleeing France whilst keeping in close touch with Rome. In many ways, this set the course of the development of the diocese, and evidence of this development can still be seen today. He was meticulous in his liturgical duties and a man of probity and sound leadership. In short, he was indeed a man who trusted in the Lord and whose soul belonged to God.

Notes

[1]　Obituary in *The Edmundian* IX:53 (1910), p. 137.

[2]　Records at University of London, Senate House Library website (accessed November 2017).

[3]　Peter Clarke, *Ryde to Rome* (Isle of Wight Catholic History Society), p. 36.

[4]　In a letter to Mowbray Baillie, 1863, widely cited, e.g. in *Gerard Manley Hopkins: A Very Private Life*, by Robert Bernard Martin.

[5]　*Isle of Wight Observer*, 6 August 1910, p. 5.

[6]　*Isle of Wight Observer*, 13 August 1910, p. 5.

[7]　Kenny, *A Path from Rome*, p. 97.

[8]　Clarke, *Ryde to Rome*, p. 55.

[9]　*Isle of Wight Observer*, 6 July 1889, p. 8.

[10]　Gerard Dwyer, *Diocese of Portsmouth: Past and Present* (Portsmouth: Portsmouth Diocesan Centenary Committee, 1981), p. 61.

[11]　Ibid., p. 64.

[12]　Ibid., p. 80.

[13]　Ibid., p. 68.

[14]　E. Greenacre and J. Haselock, *The Sacrament of Easter* (Leominster: Gracewing, 1989, 1991), pp. 101–2.

[15]　Dwyer, *Diocese of Portsmouth: Past and Present*, p. 87.

[16]　Ibid., p. 84.

[17]　*The Tablet*, 13 August 1910, p. 250.

[18]　*Isle of Wight Observer*, 13 August 1910, p. 5.

3

William Timothy Cotter (1910–40)

Cloyne is a small town in County Cork, Eire, approximately 15 miles east of the City of Cork and some three miles south of Middleton. It is barely two miles from Cork Harbour and three and a half miles from the open ocean. The economy is largely agrarian and the population in 1861 was 1,434 and by 1871 had decreased to a mere 1,235.

Its Catholic history perhaps goes back to the sixth century when *Coirpre mac Crimthainn* (*d. c.*580), King of Munster, gave land for the establishment of a monastery by St Colman (530–606), which Colman governed as abbot-bishop from 582. Cloyne was formally recognized as a diocese at the Synod of Kells in 1152 and is now a suffragan diocese in the ecclesiastical province of Cashel (also known as Munster). St Colman's Catholic Cathedral was built on an earlier foundation in about 1250.

It was here in Cloyne, in 1866, that William Timothy Cotter was born. His parents were John Cotter and Kate née Sheehan, who were both locals and were married in Cloyne on 8 August 1863. Cotter's own birth took place on 21 December and, as was the custom at the time, he was baptized the following day, 22 December 1866. His godparents are recorded as Timothy Sheehan and Ellen Sheehan. The baptism records also indicate that young William had an older brother, David John (presumably two years his senior), who was baptized, in Cloyne, on 29 December 1864. It is worth remembering that at the time of the birth of the third Bishop of Portsmouth, his future diocese did not even exist!

Little is known of Cotter's parents, but it seems his father was a naval man, following initial service in the army. Years later in life, as bishop in Portsmouth, when speaking at an event organized by the Knights of Columba, he recalled "how he had first come to Portsmouth as a small boy of eight or nine with his parents. His father was engaged on HMS

Active. His mother believed in living as near to the church as possible and in Portsmouth they were fortunate. He recalled the rector of the old Catholic chapel in Portsmouth showing them the plans of the new church."[1] Of course that new church eventually became the cathedral of the diocese of which Cotter would be bishop.

There have been 12 vessels named HMS *Active* in the Royal Navy, but the one that best fits our dates is the HMS *Active* built in the late 1860s and launched in 1869. We can discount the previous 1845 vessel which was recommissioned as a training vessel and renamed HMS *Tyne* and then HMS *Durham* in 1867. *Active* was a Volage-class corvette which entered service in 1873. She was the Commodore's ship on the Cape of Good Hope and West Africa station, and she served in both the Anglo-Ashanti and Zulu wars. In the Zulu wars, she had a crew of some 170 men and worked alongside HMS *Tenedos*, HMS *Shah* and HMS *Boadicea*. She was paid off in 1898 and sold for scrap in 1906.

Perhaps most tantalizingly there is a naval record in the Zulu wars, despatches, which in 1879 refers to promotions on HMS *Active* and includes the note that Boatswain John Cotter was promoted to Chief Boatswain.[2] Now we cannot be absolutely certain that this refers to the father of Bishop Cotter, but it seems very likely, and it underlines that John Cotter would have been abroad for much of his son's growing up. Further, there seems to be no reliable record of John Cotter's demise in UK records, suggesting perhaps that he died whilst engaged in Africa.

From these tiny details, we can imagine Cotter's father as a strong man, a role model certainly, but probably largely absent. It seems that it was Cotter's mother who looked after young William, who first taught him the faith and who sent him to church. We can imagine a close-knit household, practising the faith, and firmly guided but caring. Indeed, the small size of the Cotter household, just William and his elder brother David and their mother, is quite remarkable for an Irish family at that time and can only really be explained by the prolonged absence of Cotter's father, John.

The visit to Portsmouth, most probably around 1873 as HMS *Active* was preparing to set sail, must have been no more than that—a visit, perhaps weeks or months. Perhaps it would have been a year at the most, but what incentive would there have been for the Cotters to stay in Portsmouth once the *Active* had set sail? Furthermore, from the age of eight or so, Cotter attended the local Cloyne National School, now known as St Colman's National School. The school exists to this day and is described as a mixed mainstream primary school with a Catholic ethos.

When he was 14, Cotter went up to the much more prestigious St Colman's College in Fermoy. The land upon which the college was built was bought by Fr Timothy Murphy in 1856, who then commissioned John Pine Hurley to build the new school. The main building, built of red sandstone, is three storeys high and boasts a tower six storeys high, which has become a notable Fermoy landmark. Work was rapid and 20 months after building began the school opened its doors to students in 1858. An additional wing (1887), chapel, library and modern classrooms have all been subsequently added. The college today is one of the leading educational establishments for boys, particularly noted for its sporting prowess. The college's motto is *Dílis do Dhia agus d'Eirinn*, which might be translated as "Faithful to God and to Ireland".

At the time of Cotter's arrival, the college was a school for boarders and, in particular, it functioned as a preparatory school for the diocese of Cloyne's theological students. Records suggest that Cotter "achieved conspicuous success at the annual Intermediate Education Examination".[3]

In 1885, Cotter went up to the major seminary at Maynooth, 15 miles from Dublin, to study for the priesthood. A whole book could be (and almost certainly has been) written on the history of Maynooth, but briefly it was founded in 1795 as the national Seminary of Ireland and is formally known as the Royal College of Saint Patrick.[4] Thomas Pelham, the Chief Secretary for Ireland, introduced a bill that laid the legal foundation for the college, which was opened to train 500 priests a year and was, at one time, the largest seminary in the world.

The land for the college was donated by William Fitzgerald, the second Duke of Leinster, and the building work was paid for by the British Government. The college was also well endowed, and the first building was designed by John Stoyte. Under the rectorship of Father Laurence F. Reneham (1845–57), many further buildings were added, the most important by Augustus Pugin.

In 1875, the Second National Synod was held at Maynooth, and in 1876 the college became a constituent college of the Catholic University of Ireland, later (although after Cotter's time) offering Royal University of Ireland degrees. Later again, in 1896, Maynooth was awarded a Pontifical Charter by Pope Leo XIII, allowing the college also to award Pontifical degrees in canon law, philosophy and theology. In 1891, the new chapel designed by J. J. McCarthy was opened.

So it may be seen that at the time when young William Cotter arrived, in 1885, there was much going on at the seminary. Before we turn to the records concerning Cotter, it is worth briefly recalling how seminary formation was structured at the time. It usually lasted six years, the first two of which were spent studying philosophy, that is, scholastic philosophy based almost entirely on the writings of St Thomas Aquinas and known as "first cycle". After this came the "second cycle", a four-year study of theology, based on the key themes of the Trinity, the Incarnation, grace, redemption, the sacraments of the Church and, of course, moral theology. The most able students might have gone on to a seventh or eighth year to study at a postgraduate level.

Although a fire at Maynooth in 1940 destroyed some of the archives, the outline of Cotter's time at the seminary can be constructed from records in the college *calendarium*. He matriculated, i.e. was registered, at the college on 3 September 1885 and entered the rhetoric class, presumably a preliminary or preparatory year. The following academic year (1886–7) Cotter is recorded as a student in first philosophy. The *calendarium* for 1887–8 is missing, but in 1888–9 Cotter was in first theology and had received the tonsure. Now obsolete, the tonsure, which was the removal of a circle of hair from the back of the head, marked the formal entry into the clerical state.

In both 1889–90 and 1890–1, Cotter is listed as a student in second theology, and at the end of this sixth year, he was ordained subdeacon on 18 June 1891 by William Walsh, Archbishop of Dublin. In 1891–2, he was recorded as being in third theology and would also have been ordained to the diaconate. In the *calendarium* for 1892–3, when it would have been expected for him to be in fourth theology, he does not appear on the class list, but is recorded as having been ordained priest, again by William Walsh, Archbishop of Dublin, on 19 June 1892 (aged 25). This presumably took place in the new college chapel, completed in 1891.

So it seems that Cotter was perhaps exempt from his final year of theological study, was perhaps ordained a "year early", and according to Cotter's obituary in *The Tablet*, he was sent "to England to work on the English mission, which was then yielding insufficient English vocations to cope with the steady expansion of the church".[5] Indeed, the need in England may explain this slightly early ordination, and it seems that the situation in Portsmouth was particularly acute.

Although not relating to Cotter directly, letters from Bishop Vertue (first Bishop of Portsmouth) and in the Maynooth archive speak of a particular shortage of priests and of the deaths of priests from influenza. An extract from one of the St Patrick's College President's reports from that time also speaks of priests being ordained early to replace those who had died. So then it would seem that Cotter was ordained priest after a preliminary year and just five of the normal six years of formal study and sent to Portsmouth to assist there, partly on account of a shortage of priests. To be technical for a moment, Cotter was ordained for, and incardinated into, the Diocese of Cloyne and *loaned* to Portsmouth for six years. This explains his brief return to Ireland in 1898 (see below).

There was a small school attached to St Mary's Church in Ryde; when it expanded, Cahill invited a community of nuns (the Sisters of Mary) to come and run it, and the sisters duly arrived in October 1884. So we can see that when Cotter arrived in Ryde in 1892, he would not have found a quiet and declining parish but rather one that was vibrant and expanding, with a developing school, all directed by the far-sighted and energetic Father Cahill. By 1892, Cahill had been appointed a Domestic Prelate, Provost of the Cathedral and Protonotary Apostolic, so he must have more than welcomed the arrival of some assistance in the form of a curate, the newly ordained Fr William Cotter.

Parish records tell us he was involved in the normal round of duties for a curate: offering the Mass, officiating at weddings, burying the dead and so on. The school logbook from the time, which still exists in a bound, handwritten, but unpublished form, suggests Cotter quickly became involved in the school, visiting regularly and even teaching some of the lessons when necessary. More generally he seems to have had a particular responsibility for checking and monitoring the attendance registers. It appears that attendance was not always good and that if the weather was poor the pupils stayed away!

Also, there were clearly some issues with illness; the register entry for 26 February 1901 reads: "Attendance very poor at present owing to the prevalence of colds", and it is perhaps no surprise that academic standards were variable. Having said that, there were notable records of improvement, in addition to expressions of concern. It was Cotter who seems to have been the one to liaise with the board officer and who was significantly involved in what we would now call the management of the school. Indeed, in the later entries in the school log, he signs himself, W. T. Cotter, manager.

In 1898, Cotter returned to Cloyne and was curate at Buttevant, County Cork. In a poignant entry, Mgr Cahill recorded in the school log, on 21 September 1898, "Rev W. T. Cotter, left Ryde today. The *Isle of Wight Observer* reported that he was returning to the South of Ireland with the good wishes of many and indeed the parishioners presented him with a fine chalice.[6] However, it seems that he was not happy back in Ireland and a report in the Cloyne diocesan archive, reproduced in the Portsmouth diocesan archive, states: "He could not settle." He asked to return to the Portsmouth Diocese and permission was granted.

So, by the end of the year, the newspaper was also able to report that Mgr Cahill had announced that Fr Cotter would be returning to Ryde in the new year (i.e. early 1899), as he found Ryde more suitable for his health. He re-enters the school log on 28 March 1899, noting that the condition of the school has "fallen off". I get the impression, although the evidence is circumstantial, that Cotter did much to steer and improve the school and that this, without doubt, occupied a lot of his time.

In May 1900, Cahill was consecrated titular Bishop of Thagora, and then later in August he was appointed Bishop of Portsmouth, although according to his own diary, he continued to live in Ryde until (20 September) 1903. Having said this, the census entry for 1901 lists only a William J. Cotter (a typographical error on the initial), priest, and Catherine Molloy, a servant or housekeeper living at 7 St Mary's Passage, Ryde. Of course we can expect Bishop Cahill to have registered himself in Portsmouth, but it does open the question of exactly how much time he actually spent in Ryde and how much in Portsmouth. The *Catholic*

Directory for 1903 lists Cotter as having residences (plural) both in Portsmouth and Ryde.

Here it is also appropriate to mention Catherine Molloy, Cotter's housekeeper. The 1891 census records her living at 7 St Mary's Passage with Fr John Wallace or Wallice, who was curate at St Mary's from 1888–91, and she is described as a widow and "general servant, domestic" from Kilkenny, Ireland. In the 1901 census, the description is the same, but she now lives with Cotter as his housekeeper. A notice in the *Isle of Wight Observer* records the death of Catherine Molloy on 26 March 1910, aged 82 years, in St Mary's Presbytery in Ryde. She is buried in Ryde cemetery, although her tombstone records her age as 83. Either way, she was no doubt a faithful old lady who had served the priests of Ryde for many years. Buried with Catherine is her daughter Mary Molloy, who died at Bishop's House, Portsmouth on 9 April 1931, aged 75. So it appears that both mother and daughter served Cotter, the latter moving with him to Portsmouth when he was appointed diocesan bishop in 1910.

Cotter succeeded Cahill as rector of Ryde (in 1900) and was confirmed as bishop's secretary. Cotter's obituary informs us that "his practical gifts, his force of character and grasp of business marked him out early for diocesan tasks". He was also described as "a man of singularly striking presence and a fine type of the Irish parish priest, at once apostolic, authoritative and charitable with a warmth of human feeling and native humour".[7] Small wonder then, that within a mere ten years of ordination, he had a canonry conferred upon him. The *Isle of Wight Observer* noted that "The Rev Cotter, so well-known and respected, has been made a canon whereat the congregation of St Mary's are extremely pleased."[8] Additionally, the school records tell us that on 2 July 1902 the Revd W. T. Cotter distributed good conduct medals, but on 1 September 1902, the school received a visit from the Very Revd Canon W. T. Cotter, who distributed good conduct medals the following day.

As rector in Ryde, Cotter's work carried on largely as before, but he was no doubt busier and had to bear more responsibility. Also, of course, he was assistant and secretary to Bishop Cahill, and whilst this was good preparation for his future, it must have kept him busy. He continued to work very closely with the school, and there are entries by Cotter in the logbook right up until the end of 1904, just months before he was consecrated bishop. Furthermore, from 1899 until 1905 he did not have a curate, perhaps because Bishop Cahill was living with him on and off and there being insufficient space in the presbytery. When Cotter was made auxiliary bishop and continued to live in Ryde, he did have a number of curates who must have run the parish on a day-to-day basis: Fr Thomas O'Connor from 1905–6; Fr Laurence Farelly from 1906–7; Fr William Flynn from 1907–9, and Fr Patrick McSwiney, who arrived in 1909 and stayed until 1912.

As I mentioned above, towards the end of his life Bishop Cahill did not enjoy good health. In 1904, he became seriously ill, and all hope of recovery had been given up. Nevertheless, Cahill did survive, but prompted by his poor health, he somewhat unusually applied to Rome that Cotter might be appointed his auxiliary. Pope Pius X agreed to Cahill's request and Cotter was appointed titular bishop of Clazomenae and auxiliary bishop of Portsmouth on 14 February 1905. He was consecrated in Portsmouth Cathedral on 19 March (the feast of St Joseph) by Cahill, assisted by George Burton, Bishop of Clifton and Peter Amigo, Bishop of Southwark.

We can see that Cotter quickly took on many of the important diocesan tasks, and he is notably representing Cahill in Jersey in 1905. It is perhaps no surprise that this very early visit was to the Irish mission established at St Mary and St Peter's Church there. The building of Fort Regent at the beginning of the nineteenth century had brought a number of Irish labourers to Jersey. Originally, they went to Mass at the French Chapel in Castle Street, but in time the combined French and Irish communities outgrew the accommodation, and there is also some suggestion that they did not always get on, and a separate Irish mission was established, and indeed grew and flourished. All the details need not concern us here, but a new (albeit incomplete!) church was opened in 1867. There were problems paying off the associated debts, but this was finally achieved by Fr John Hourigan, and Bishop Cotter visited and consecrated the church in 1905. It should be noted that the Church of St Mary and St Peter that we speak of here was the original and should not be confused with the modern church, on a separate site, that replaced it.

As an aside, while considering the Channel Islands, it is also appropriate to note that Bishop Cotter visited Guernsey in 1934. This visit is particularly notable since, it is said, it was the first time that a British bishop had travelled *by air* on an official visitation. Rough seas in the Channel prevented him taking the ferry and so he flew to Guernsey.

In 1906, the first Church of St David, East Cowes, on the Isle of Wight was erected in Connaught Road and was described as a tiny iron church. It is remarkable that some 150 people squeezed in to attend the Pontifical High Mass celebrated by Bishop Cotter at the opening. A later brick-built church (1923) replaced the iron church, although it was itself destroyed in a bombing raid in May 1942.

Bishop Cotter had a high-profile role at Farnborough Abbey in 1908. The Abbey of Saint Michael was commissioned by the ex-Empress Eugenie, and designed by Gabriel Destailleur, as a mausoleum for her husband Emperor Napoleon III and her son, the Prince Imperial. The splendid church in French Gothic and Romanesque styles (now Grade I listed) was opened by Bishop Vertue in 1887 and originally served by Premonstratensian Canons (Norbertines). However, in 1896, the abbey was taken over by French Benedictines from Solesmes and Dom Fernand Cabrol was elected the first abbot. The abbey quickly became a centre of liturgical excellence and scholarship. In 1908, Bishop Cotter consecrated the abbey church. *The Tablet* reported that "as would be expected, the function was carried out in the most complete manner ... one of the features of the [consecration] service, and a very rare one these days, was that it concluded with sung Terce and Solemn Mass celebrated by the consecrating bishop. The service began at 8am and ended at 1.15pm."[9]

Bishop Cotter was back at Farnborough Abbey for the funeral of Empress Eugenie on 20 July 1920. Dom Cabrol, OSB, the Abbot, sang the Requiem Mass and Bishop Cotter officiated at the burial in the imperial crypt. *The Tablet* asked: "When again shall a Benedictine Abbot on English soil receive three anointed kings at his church door?" And went on to describe the Benedictine chant which "rose as simple in melody as the monotonous light thrown by the stark yellow candles ... for the first time since Catherine of Aragon, the royalty of England and Spain heard Mass together".[10] This has been described as "Cotter's finest hour", for the whole ceremony took place in the presence of King George V and Queen Mary, and the largest gathering of European royalty ever to assemble in a Catholic church in England.

In 1902, Cotter went to Rome for the first time and was received by Pope Leo XIII. Again, in 1908, Cotter also accompanied Bishop Cahill on a visit to Rome for the celebrations of the golden jubilee of the priesthood of Pope Pius X. On 31 October 1908, *The Tablet's* Rome correspondent reported that

> The English day at the Vatican began on Monday morning, by the private audience granted by the Holy Father to the new auditor of the sacred Roman Rota, Mgr John Prior . . . Immediately afterwards the Pope left his private library and proceeded to the Throne Room where he granted audience to the Archbishop of Westminster, Archbishop Stonor, Bishop Giles the Bishop of Birmingham, the Bishop of Portsmouth, the Bishop of Northampton, the Bishop of Nottingham, Bishop Cotter, Bishop Collins and Bishop Lenihan of Auckland . . . each of them was permitted to kiss the Holy Father's ring, and all followed him into the *Sala Regia* where a throne had been erected and round it chairs for the members of the Episcopate.[11]

Later, on 8 November, there was another report of the reception of Cahill and Cotter and other English bishops by Pope Pius X and these bishops along with many, many others were present for the Jubilee Mass celebrated in St Peter's. *The Tablet* observed that "perhaps never since the Vatican Council have there been so many English bishops in Rome at the same time".[12] This report is poignantly underlined by the observation, two weeks later, that "the halls of the Pope's apartments were silent and empty".[13]

Perhaps the last major event that Cotter attended as auxiliary bishop, and therefore a representative of Bishop Cahill, was the consecration of Westminster Cathedral on 28 June 1910. *The Tablet* reported it was a "celebration which will go down as one of the greatest and most moving in our history". The archbishop consecrated the cathedral and then the Mass was "celebrated by Bishop Cotter in the presence of the Archbishop, the Bishops, Monsignori, Canons, Cathedral Chaplains, Superiors of Religious Orders, almost 200 clergy secular and regular and a vast concourse of people". We can imagine a vast and complex celebration, presided over by Cotter on this occasion, and again *The Tablet* also observed that "the greatest day the cathedral has seen or will ever see passed into history".[14]

On 2 August 1910, Bishop Cahill died, and on 24 November Cotter was confirmed as the third Bishop of Portsmouth. He took the episcopal motto *Non recuso laborem* ("I will not refuse work") and chose a coat of arms depicting a Celtic cross and three shamrocks in gold, on a green background. *The Tablet* described him as The Right Reverend William T. Cotter D.D., and observes that his elevation corresponded with the general expectation.[15] Fr John Henry King, who studied in Rome and who had succeeded Cotter as Bishop Cahill's secretary, (when Cotter was elevated to the purple in 1905) now became Cotter's secretary until he (King) was appointed to be parish priest of Winchester in 1923.

In 1910, Bishop Cotter moved to Portsmouth and, now in charge of the diocese, made a number of changes to the cathedral. In 1912, he erected a set of Stations of the Cross in memory of Bishop Cahill, and in 1924 the St Patrick Chapel was added to the north side, again in memory of Bishop Cahill, and particularly in thanksgiving for his completion of the cathedral. This chapel was not part of the original plan and contains stained glass by Nathaniel Westlake, depicting scenes from the life of St Patrick, which was originally in the wall of the north aisle.

I have noted above Cotter's unflagging commitment to the primary school in Ryde. As bishop, it would seem that his commitment to education generally and Catholic education in particular continued. In 1911, he organized a "School Children's Demonstration", when Catholic schoolchildren attended the cathedral *en masse*, for a special service. "Marshalled by their clergy and teachers upon the Naval Recreation Ground, they marched in procession, through the crowded thoroughfares to the cathedral . . . the imposing procession was headed by the bishop." Pontifical benediction followed the procession, and the bishop provided the children with refreshments! *The Tablet* described this as a "novel function",[16] but it must have done much to boost and promote Catholic education within the diocese, and it strongly suggests Cotter's commitment to it.

And it was not only schoolchildren. The bishop is also recorded, later in 1911, as having presided at a meeting of the Catholic Needlework

Guild on the occasion that the Portsmouth Division were celebrating their silver jubilee. Cotter gave a short address encouraging the ladies in their work and he gave his blessing to all present.

In 1912, Cotter would make his own *ad limina* visit to Rome and was received by Pope Pius X again. We know little of the visit, but on his return to Portsmouth crowds of well-wishers gathered in their thousands to welcome him home. Mr FitzPatrick Boxell read a formal welcome address in the name of the whole Catholic community and after the gathering the assembled crowd proceeded to the cathedral where a solemn *Te Deum* was sung, to give thanks for Cotter's safe return. Cotter gave benediction to conclude the event, and some days later, on the Sunday in the Octave of St Edmund of Abingdon (feast day 17 November) imparted the papal blessing.

Of course, Cotter was also bishop in Portsmouth throughout the First World War. Whilst Portsmouth is home to the Royal Navy, it is easy to overlook the fact that at the very beginning of the twentieth century it was considered as the world's greatest naval port, and the British Empire was at its zenith. In 1900, Portsmouth dockyard employed 8,000 men. With the onset of the First World War, the port became even busier, refitting some 1,200 ships, and the workforce almost tripled. This, however, meant that Portsmouth was a key target for the enemy, and the Germans claimed that the city was heavily bombarded by a Zeppelin airship on 1 October 1916. However, there were no British reports of any bombs dropped in this area, although there were some claims that the munitions had fallen into the sea.

It is widely recognized that Bishop Cahill did much to encourage religious orders and foundations to establish themselves in the new Diocese of Portsmouth. Furthermore, it is widely acknowledged that Bishop Cotter did little to expand this work, but that he did much to consolidate it. Benedictine monks from Solesmes in France came to the Isle of Wight in 1901, settling at Appuldurcombe House near Wroxall. With encouragement from Bishop Cahill, they moved to Quarr Abbey House in 1907, acquiring land that was home to the ruins of a medieval Cistercian house suppressed by Henry VIII in 1537. The monk-architect Dom Paul Bellot designed and directed the building of the new abbey. The building of the new abbey church was begun in 1911 and completed the following year. On Saturday 11 October 1912, Bishop Cotter consecrated five altars assisted by the bishops of Quimper and Langres and the Abbots of Farnborough and St Martin's, Liguge. "The impressive consecration ceremonies occupied nearly six hours, the whole concluding with Pontifical High Mass ... after the ceremony a peal of bells from Solesmes was rung for the first time."[17]

St Dominic's Priory at Carisbrooke, near Newport on the Isle of Wight, was founded by Elizabeth Countess of Clare in 1866 as a community of Dominican nuns. Celebrations to mark their golden jubilee in 1916, included the consecration of their chapel by Bishop Cotter. Entering the chapel the bishop traced alpha and omega—the first and last letters of the Greek alphabet—in ashes, which had been strewn on the floor. He blessed the chapel inside and out and formally consecrated the whole in honour of Our Lady of Reparation and St Dominic. "The nuns' voices rang out around the chapel as the bishop sang Pontifical High Mass." Although no longer a convent, the twelve consecration sconces may still be seen in the chapel to this day.

In 1922, the Benedictine nuns of *Pax Cordis Jesu* at Ventnor (founded 1882) moved to St Cecilia's Abbey in Appley near Ryde which had been vacated by the exiled Solesmes nuns who had returned to France the previous year. The abbey bells were blessed in 1923, and the second, the Gulielmus-Clara Bell, was in honour of Bishop Cotter and Mme Claire de Livron (mother of Mère Ambrosia). In 1926, the priory was formally raised to the status of an abbey, and it was Bishop Cotter who presided over the election of a new abbess at which Mère Ambrosia was unanimously elected (succeeding Mère Placide). Following the election, Bishop Cotter returned to the abbey to confer the abbatial blessing on Mère Ambrosia, on 26 April. This was one of many visits, and records show Bishop Cotter presided at some 30 professions. In 1950, the community was formally aggregated to the Solesmes congregation.

In June 1917, Cotter concluded what might be described as the first phase of his life as a bishop, celebrating his own silver jubilee of ordination to the priesthood. "Congratulations flowed in from all quarters of the diocese and from various parts of England and Ireland, and in the presence of a large congregation he celebrated his Jubilee Mass in the cathedral."[18]

The depression between the world wars was predominantly a time for consolidation rather than new ventures and expansion. Indeed, Bishop Cotter himself referred to his own work as "consolidation of the work done by his predecessors".[19] Many debts on church buildings were paid off, and churches were completed, opened or consecrated, but new parishes and new buildings were rare in this period—particularly in comparison to the rapid and widespread expansion of churches and parishes in the diocese under Bishop Cahill (1900–10).

In fact, within the city of Portsmouth only one new parish was established (and church built) during the episcopate of Bishop Cotter. In 1921, a Mrs Collins and a Mrs Clarke approached Bishop Cotter for permission to start collecting for a church in Cosham. Permission was granted and Fr Francis Stanford, a curate at the cathedral, was put in charge of the new district. The church was built, and Bishop Cotter blessed and opened the new church dedicated to St Colman on 25 November 1928. This is the feast of St Colman, but Bishop Cotter also pointed out in his homily that this dedication was fitting, because of the large number of priests and people who had migrated from Cloyne to the City of Portsmouth.

Again, in terms of consolidation, Bishop Cotter did not invite religious orders to establish themselves in the diocese in the way that his predecessor had done. In 1910, Bishop Cahill invited the Sisters of Our Lady of Charity, a French-founded order which first came to England in 1863, to the diocese. They established themselves in Waterlooville, where, at the time, there was only one Catholic family, the Harcourts. The sisters specialized in the care of wayward girls who were in danger of losing the faith. The sisters' dream was to build a chapel next to their Convent of St Michael, and they began to raise money by running a laundry. The First World War intervened again, and it was not until after the conflict that plans were drawn up, again by architect W. C. Mangen, to build a chapel. Here Bishop Cotter intervened. He requested that the Romanesque chapel be built in such a way that the chapel could be used by the sisters, by those for whom they were caring and the increasing number of Catholics in the area until such time as a parish church could be built for them. This accounts for the triple-aisle design of the chapel. The new chapel, of St Michael, was opened by Bishop Cotter on 6 December 1923.

In 1973, the convent and the parish celebrated the golden jubilee of the chapel, now a statutory Grade II listed building, but a new parish church, dedicated to the Sacred Heart, was eventually built, and dedicated by Bishop Crispian Hollis (seventh of Portsmouth) in 2011. The original chapel still exists but is no longer open for public worship.

The Catholic community in Totland, at the extreme west end of the Isle of Wight, flourished for many years and was, from 1871, centred on the private chapel in Weston Manor, home of the Ward family. "In 1888 the chapel was decorated in a medieval style, after the designs of the famous 'glossary' of Mr A. W. Pugin, and is the only example of its kind in England."[20] When Mr. E. G. Ward died in 1915, he bequeathed £5,000 for the construction of a new parish church, which was designed by architects James H. Mangan and Wilfrid C. Mangan of Preston, with Mr Frank Privett as builder. The church is built of red brick, with round arched Romanesque windows, and has a distinctive tower. Bishop Cotter formally blessed and opened the church with a High Mass on 14 August 1923. The bishop's ten-page sermon included: "This is your church— your spiritual home. It belongs to each of you—cherish it, love it and above all use it!"[21] When all the debts had been paid off, Bishop John King (fourth Bishop of Portsmouth) consecrated the church on 23 May 1954.

The Catholic community in Winchester has a long and venerable history and the practice of the Catholic religion endured through much of the Reformation. In 1901, Bishop Cahill wrote that a new church in Winchester was soon to be commenced, based on a building fund left by the late Fr Ignatius Collingridge. Canon Luke Gunning took the work forward, encouraged by the Pope, no less, but the First World War intervened again, and it would be some 25 years until the building of the new St Peter's Church was properly underway. The building was commenced and the foundation stone laid on 1 February 1924 by Bishop Cotter, who returned to open the church on the feast of St Swithun in 1926. (St Swithun was the ninth-century bishop of Winchester who was traditionally celebrated on 15 July, but whose feast day is now kept on 2 July.)

It is said that during his time at Ryde, and presumably beyond, Cotter was a regular visitor to Ireland. In 1920, he is recorded as having been present at the funeral of Canon Maurice O'Callaghan, the late parish priest of Cloyne. In October 1933, he attended the centenary celebrations at Mount Melleray Abbey in County Waterford and celebrated a Pontifical High Mass there. His Irish connections are further underlined by a report of Bishop Cotter's attendance at the Knights of St Columba's St Patrick's Day dinner in 1927. In a speech, it was said that "they admired his Lordship for the wonderful example he set them all, they reverenced him as their bishop and most of all they loved him for his charming personality".[22] In his reply, the bishop made a reference to a leak in a newspaper and joked that the Grand National winner might be similarly leaked. He also made reference to their shared faith, given to them through St Patrick. There can be little doubt of Bishop Cotter's devotion to all things Irish, even horse-racing!

The origins of the Catholic mission in Sandown are uncertain, but Fr De Mainvilliers became Sandown's first resident priest, saying Mass at the Albert Road Chapel. In 1914, Fr Flynn proposed the building of a permanent chapel, but due to the First World War the project was delayed. This perhaps explains the remark in Canon Scantlebury's *Catholic Story of The Isle of Wight* where he says, "it has not been possible to obtain any information about the Mission at Sandown or of the church said to have been built there in 1908".[23]

The persistent Fr Flynn did not give up, however. In 1928, the foundation of the new church was finally laid and the church was opened in June the following year. The architect was W. C. Mangan of Preston, and the Romanesque design was closely modelled on Honan Chapel in Gillabbey, County Cork. This church, designed by James McCullen, was a major work in the Irish Arts and Crafts movement which would most probably have been known to Cotter. The Sandown church is also notable for the Irish stained glass by the Harry Clarke Studios of Dublin.

Indeed, Cotter may well have encouraged the building of this Irish-styled church, and doubtless he would not have opposed the dedication to St Patrick. By all accounts, when he consecrated the church in 1938, it was a magnificent celebration. The *Portsmouth Evening News* spoke of an impressive ancient ritual, involving music, anointing of 12 consecration crosses and blessings with holy water. The ceremony began at 8.30 in the morning and lasted over three hours.

Bournemouth expanded rapidly at the end of the nineteenth and in the early part of the twentieth century, and Catholic life flourished and expanded too. The Church of the Annunciation, designed by Sir Giles Gilbert Scott, was opened in the northern district of the city by Bishop Cahill in 1907. There was a period of consolidation during the years of the First World War, but in 1932 Corpus Christi Church in Boscombe, which was originally founded in 1895, was considerably enlarged and the extended church was solemnly blessed by Bishop Cotter on 22 April 1934.

Also in 1934, Bishop Cotter created a new parish of Southbourne and Fr (later Canon) Jesse Hetherington was appointed the first parish priest. A plot of land had been acquired, and Fr Hetherington lost no time in building first a presbytery and then the Church of Our Lady Queen of Peace. The foundation stone was laid on 8 September 1938, and the church opened the following May.

In 1930, Cotter celebrated his episcopal silver jubilee, and received a number of congratulatory letters and telegrams, including one from Rome, sent by Cardinal Pacelli (later Pope Pius XII) imparting the Holy Father's Apostolic Blessing. In 1935, Cotter was celebrating 25 years as Bishop of Portsmouth, by coincidence in the same year that the English martyrs Ss John Fisher and Thomas More (22 June) were canonized by Pope Pius XI. Cotter was conscious of the sacrifices made by the English martyrs and frequently spoke of their witness.

Towards the end of his life, Bishop Cotter suffered from ill health and spent some of his time being cared for at the Esperance Nursing Home in Eastbourne in Sussex. He requested that his former secretary and by then vicar general, Canon John Henry King, be appointed as his auxiliary. Bishop Cotter died in his sleep on Thursday evening, 24 October 1940 at Bishop's House in Portsmouth. His death was described as sudden but not unexpected following illness. According to his death certificate, the cause of death was myocardial degeneration and senility. He was 73 years old and the second oldest prelate in the British Catholic hierarchy (after Bishop Amigo) at that time.

In his will, which was written in 1933 and executed by Bishop King, he left his estate to the Revd J. H. King, the Very Revd Patrick Joseph O'Leary (sometime of Southsea) and Canon Francis Joseph Murphy (sometime of Ventnor), although, in the event, the latter two predeceased him. Cotter's estate was valued at £5,434 19s 8d, (gross), which attracted death duty of £201 6s 10d. It would appear that Cotter had made a few shrewd investments, and there are records in the diocesan archive of Cotter having held shares in Harrods!

On Sunday 27 October, in the afternoon, his coffin was taken to the cathedral to allow mourners to pay their final respects. On Tuesday 29 October at 11.30 a.m., a solemn requiem was sung by Bishop King in the presence of the Apostolic Delegate, Archbishop Godfrey, "who presided in *Cappa Magna* at the throne".[24] The cathedral was crowded to the doors with thousands outside the church. There can be little doubt that Bishop Cotter, who had been Bishop of Portsmouth for 30 years, was held in great affection. Indeed, in letters and telegrams of condolence one wrote, "I have lost one of my oldest and dearest friends" and another wrote of a "beloved and distinguished churchman".

After the requiem, Bishop King buried Bishop Cotter at the Convent cemetery in Waterlooville. Many priests of the diocese, and nuns also, joined the procession from the cathedral to the cemetery: a procession which was "three quarters of a mile long".[25] Portsmouth's first Catholic Lord Mayor, Cllr D. A. Daley, made the following tribute following Cotter's death:

> He was the embodiment of all that Christianity stood for. He radiated kindness, and that coupled with a ready and generous Irish wit, made him the friend of all who came in to contact with him. To all Catholics of his diocese he was a father in the true sense of the word. In this respect he was capable when stern action was demanded of administering rebuke besides praise. His illness was nobly borne and if ever suffering was angelic it was with him. He would smile through pain.[26]

So then to conclude, how best may we summarize Cotter's life and what was his legacy? I think first and foremost Bishop Cotter was more than true to his episcopal motto: "I will not refuse work." He worked tirelessly as bishop for 30 years, strengthening the diocese and building upon the foundations his predecessors had laid. The number of churches that he blessed, opened and consecrated in some solemn and very lengthy liturgies is remarkable, and this short biographical account has mentioned only a selection. In one obituary, he was described as impressive and eloquent: one who loved ceremonies and indeed, as I have noted, it was Cotter who presided at the first Pontifical High Mass in Westminster Cathedral following its consecration in 1910 and who officiated at the burial of Empress Eugenie in the presence of massed ranks of European royalty. Further, Cotter was no stay-at-home cleric and travelled widely across the diocese, to Ireland regularly and to Rome.

The second obvious and unavoidable characteristic of Bishop Cotter was his nationality: his inescapable "Irishness". As bishop, he did not hesitate to use his own influence and authority. On one of his very first excursions, he visited the Irish mission in Jersey. He added the St Patrick's Chapel to the cathedral; he had the new church in Cosham dedicated to St Colman, the Cloyne Saint from his boyhood, and he encouraged and furthered the building of the church in Sandown, not only dedicated to St Patrick, but modelled on an Irish church and containing Irish stained glass. Two of the three beneficiaries of his will, had they outlived him, were Irishmen. Finally, it is also alleged that at the end of every public Mass which he celebrated as bishop, he required the congregation to sing "O glorious St Patrick, dear Saint of our isle". Perhaps this is more anecdote than fact, but it points again to Cotter's deep-seated Irish identity.

It is also worth noting that Cotter was a loyal servant of the pope. He went to Rome three times (at least) and met several popes. The Portsmouth diocesan archive contains a considerable correspondence between him and various offices and officials in Rome. Much of it, written in Latin, points to a close relationship at the time between Portsmouth and the Holy See. Furthermore, correspondence between Cotter and Cardinal Bourne (Archbishop of Westminster) points to a close relationship with the English hierarchy too.

Lastly, it seems that Bishop Cotter was a genial and friendly bishop, well liked by both his priests and people. The genuine warmth, expressed in correspondence with Cotter, especially on significant anniversaries, and the genuine grief expressed at his death indicate that he really was a much-loved man. My own feeling is that this came to a large extent from him being what a bishop should be and doing what a bishop should do: preaching, teaching and leading his diocese—but ruling with care and affection, tirelessly travelling to all parts of the diocese, and being present at many major events. His final illness must have been a great trial to him, but, as Cllr Daley attested, he bore it bravely. He was a great asset to the Church and to his diocese, which he served so well. For the record, he is still the longest-serving Bishop of Portsmouth.

Notes

[1] Gerard Dwyer, *Diocese of Portsmouth: Past and Present* (Portsmouth: Portsmouth Diocesan Centenary Committee, 1981), pp. 88–9; *Portsmouth Evening News*, 28 October 1940.

[2] J. Grehan and M. Mace, *The Zulu War* (Barnsley: Pen & Sword, 2013), p. 229.

[3] Dwyer, *Diocese of Portsmouth Past and Present*, p. 89.

[4] See, for example, Patrick Corish, *Maynooth College, 1795 to 1995* (Dublin: Gill & Macmillan, 1994).

[5] *The Tablet*, 2 November 1940, p. 350.

[6] Cf. *Isle of Wight Observer*, 19 November 1898.

[7] *The Tablet*, 2 November 1940, p. 350.

[8] *Isle of Wight Observer*, 4 October 1902.

[9] *The Tablet*, 17 October 1908, p. 635.

[10] *The Tablet*, 24 July 1920, p. 112.

[11] *The Tablet*, 31 October 1908, p. 699.

[12] *The Tablet*, 21 November 1908.

[13] *The Tablet*, 6 December 1908.

[14] *The Tablet*, 2 July 1910, p. 6 and p. 33.

[15] Cf. *The Tablet*, 3 December 1910, p. 889–90.

[16] *The Tablet*, 29 July 1911, p. 179.

[17] *Portsmouth Evening News*, 14 October 1912.

[18] Dwyer, *Diocese of Portsmouth: Past and Present*, p. 89.

19   *Portsmouth Evening News*, 18 March 1927.

20   *St. Saviour's R.C. Church and Community*, p. 5.

21   Ibid., p. 9.

22   *Portsmouth Evening News*, 18 March 1927.

23   R. E. Scantlebury, *The Catholic Story of the Isle of Wight* (Havant: Pelham, 1962), p. 86.

24   *Portsmouth Evening News*, 29 October 1940.

25   *Portsmouth Evening News*, 30 October 1940.

26   Dwyer, *Diocese of Portsmouth: Past and Present*, p. 103, quoting the *Portsmouth Evening News*.

4

John Henry King (1941–65)

John Henry King was born on 16 September 1880 at Westfield Farm, Wardour, Salisbury in Wiltshire. He was presumably named after Newman who had been created Cardinal Deacon of San Giorgio in Valabro by Pope Leo XIII the year before. His father, a farmer, was John Frederick King and his mother was Mary Lucy née Darley. He had several sisters.

He grew up on the land and had the practical wisdom of those who know the rigours of farming. He first heard Mass in the chapel choir loft, standing knee-high to his father who sang tenor. According to *The Diocese of Portsmouth Past and Present*, he attended the Dames' School in the Cathedral Close, Salisbury. The cathedral dates back to the thirteenth century, and incidentally, the cathedral close at Salisbury is the largest in the country. In the eighteenth and nineteenth centuries, dames' schools were small (independent) infant-cum-junior schools run by one or more "school dames" who taught the basics of education for a modest fee, and according to D. P. Leinster-Maclay's article in the *British Journal of Educational Studies*, while some were very good, some were "travesties of schools even by nineteenth century standards".[1] In Salisbury, at the time, there were some dozen or so dames' schools.

As he was a Catholic, it may be, in fact, that young John Henry's Salisbury school was St Osmund's, which possibly began as a dames' school and is located in Exeter Street, a road off the Cathedral Close. In 1886, the income for the school derived from 18 boys, 12 girls and 21 infants, but in 1888 the school received a grant from the State. St Osmund's is a Catholic primary school to this day.

Devotional practices were instilled into the young boy from an early age by his grandmother, with whom he lived while attending school in Salisbury:

> As soon as the midday meal was over on a Sunday, things had to be cleared away lest visitors should arrive. Then grandmother would get the young John Henry and his aunt Mary to help her with her night prayers as she herself sat upright in a high backed chair, while the boy and his aunt sat on the floor . . . His grandmother's night prayers finished just in time to allow aunt Mary to take John Henry to Vespers, Sermon and Benediction at St Osmund's Church.[2]

After Salisbury, he went to a school run by the Sisters of Mercy in Abingdon, Oxfordshire, founded in 1860 and now known as Our Lady's, Abingdon, an independent school for boys and girls. From Abingdon, he went as a lay pupil to the College of St Mary, Woolhampton, latterly Douai Abbey School (which closed in 1999). It is said that he was always grateful for the education that he received there, especially in commercial subjects and mathematics.

After he left school, he began working at a bookseller's shop in Salisbury. Having discerned a vocation to the priesthood, John Henry applied to his former college at Douai, where he was admitted as a student for the priesthood for the Diocese of Portsmouth. After a year at Douai, he was sent in 1889 to the Venerable English College in Rome. At this time, William Giles was the rector, who had done much to improve the college's finances and complete the new chapel, as vice-rector under his predecessor Henry O'Callaghan, who had been appointed Bishop of Hexham and Newcastle.

O'Callaghan was a strict disciplinarian, but Giles was a genial man and adopted a more easy-going approach with the students, taking part in their Christmas concerts and accompanying them on walking tours in the hill towns near Rome. He found it difficult to correct students and enforce rules. Furthermore, on the intellectual front, modernism was in the air. This was a rather diffuse Catholic movement that endorsed contemporary biblical criticism and questioned the role of neo-scholasticism. embracing developments in contemporary science and philosophy.

One of the main representatives of modernism was Alfred Loisy (1857–1940), and King recalled in his diary that during a discussion of the translation of Loisy's book *L'évangile et l'église* the opinion was expressed that it was full of error. Loisy had got hold of false principles of philosophy and was applying them to matters of faith, causing havoc. King also reported in his diary on 7 January 1901 that Prior, that is to say Mgr John Prior, the vice-rector of the *Venerabile*, gave an address to the students warning them against modernist liberal Catholicism, which he said would, at the very least, dull the fire of their attachment to the vicar of Christ.[3]

Bishop John Baptist Cahill recalled King from Rome shortly before the conclusion of his studies, supposedly fearful of the modernist scare and lest he be "contaminated". In the same vein, after his ordination, Bishop Cahill apparently said to the new priest, "You have heard the old saying set a thief to catch a thief, well you will now examine the newly ordained priests to see if they are tainted with modernism."[4]

By this time, Bishop Cahill was quite seriously ill, and too ill to ordain King, and so he was sent, with William Flynn, to be ordained priest for the Diocese of Portsmouth on 20 November 1904 at St Helier in Jersey by Bishop Jules Prosper Paris SJ (1846–1931), a French bishop and Vicar Apostolic of Nanking.

On account of his poor health, Bishop Cahill took the unusual step, at the time, of applying to Rome for an auxiliary bishop, and Cahill's secretary William Cotter was duly appointed. King in turn, following his ordination, was appointed as Bishop Cahill's new secretary. The role of a bishop's secretary is to assist the bishop in all aspects of his ministry, not just manage his correspondence and his diary. The secretary therefore is privy to much sensitive and confidential information and so must be the soul of discretion. Hence, we really do not know a great deal about the early years of King's priestly life.

However, we do know that in 1904 the Catholic Record Society was founded and started to publish the *Catholic Register*. It is said that the young Fr King read avidly all the CRS volumes and soon became an expert on recusant history (with a special interest in the English Martyrs). Those interested in the subject frequently turned to Fr King for information. It is said that Bishop King was never much of a conversationalist and uninterested in small talk, but if the conversation turned to Catholic history, he became animated and could hold his audience spellbound by the depth and breadth of his knowledge. Indeed, as bishop, he was for many years president of the Catholic Record Society. His published works are minimal, but he filled many exercise books with pencil jottings and notes.

In 1910 Bishop Cahill died, and Bishop Cotter succeeded him as the third Bishop of Portsmouth. Fr King then became Cotter's secretary, a post he held for a further 13 years. We have already seen what a busy and energetic bishop Cotter was, and Fr King must have been kept very busy too.

In 1923, King was appointed parish priest of Winchester, which has a Catholic history going back to around 1674, when the layman Roger Corham "founded the parish". Corham had wanted to be a priest, but having killed a man in a duel he was ineligible and so did all he could to build up the faith as a layman. Mass was celebrated in a room in his house in St Peter Street, and he installed a resident priest. Later, as the congregation grew, he converted his garden shed into a makeshift chapel and indeed enlarged it twice. The Second Catholic Relief Act of 1791 made it possible to build a proper church, and in 1792 Dr (later Bishop) John Milner replaced the chapel with a building in the Gothic Revival style. King himself succeeded Fr Ignatius Collingridge and Fr Luke Gunning, who between them had cared for and served the Catholics of Winchester for almost 80 years (1847–1923). As early as 1901, there had been talk of a new church in Winchester; Bishop Cahill mentioned it in his Rosary Sunday letter of that year, but for various reasons, not least the First World War, and despite there being the nucleus of a building fund left by Fr Collingridge, there was no new church.

It was Fr King who finally set to work to build the new church, replacing Milner's 1792 church. The work began on 24 February 1924 to a design by the London ecclesiastical architect Frederick A. Walters in the Gothic Revival style. The church was built by Mussellwhite's of Basingstoke at a cost of £30,000, and it was blessed on the evening of 14

July by Bishop Cotter and opened the following day, 15 July 1926. *The Tablet* reported:

> When one speaks now of the Catholic church of St Peter, Winchester, the reference is no longer to the simply planned but in its day notable structure erected by Milner during his pastorate in this Hampshire city, but to the new handsome, more spacious building which was opened with due solemnity last week, on the feast of St Swithun, by his Lordship the Bishop of Portsmouth, in the presence of His Eminence Cardinal Bourne who preached the opening Sermon.

Amongst other things Bourne said:

> I am delighted to share the joy of the Catholics of this city who, after many anticipations, so much long hope, have now the realization of the building and opening of this beautiful church. From my heart I congratulate the bishop of this diocese and his clergy, and all Catholics of this city, and if I venture to congratulate the city itself on the building of this church, the presence of the Mayor, Aldermen and Councillors show that my words may be taken in good part.

When all the costs associated with the building of the church had been met, the church was consecrated by Bishop King himself on 22 September 1938. The church is Grade II listed.

A number of features of the church are particularly connected with Fr King. The windows in the north wall of the Lady Chapel

> commemorate five of the martyrs who were executed for their faith in the late 16th century. Designed and made by Arthur Edward Buss of Goddard and Gibbs in 1967, they are a memorial from the parish to Archbishop King who is depicted in the glass. The wild flowers along the bottom borders reflect his love of gardens and of the Hampshire countryside.

Also in the Lady Chapel is a fifteenth-century carved statue of the Madonna and Child discovered in a Canterbury antique shop by the architect in 1927. It was restored professionally and presented to the parish by Canon King as a memorial to Fr Collingridge. On the other side of the church is the Sacred Heart Chapel which was installed to mark the silver jubilee of the church. The altar and screen were consecrated by Bishop King on the feast of the Sacred Heart 1951.[5]

Fr King remained as parish priest in Winchester for 12 years. In addition to his growing interest in Catholic history and archive work, and his work to build the new church, he also became involved, first hand as it were, with the archives and historical ephemera at Winchester, said by some to be the best archives of any parish in the diocese. King wrote a report on his findings in 1930. In addition to a box of treasurers under Canon Gunning's bed, in the library-cum-sitting room on the first floor, which Fr King named the "glory hole", he found liturgical silverware, old altar stones, vestments and various handwritten sermons and other documents. In another house, the White House, given to the parish and part of the parish complex and at one time a convent, Fr King found more articles. He recorded:

> During the short, bleak days of January my investigations proceeded. After removing crowds of old vestments, boxes of clothes, books belonging to a former curate, school models, tables, old chairs etc. . . . at length I came to the books, books everywhere. The walls and floor were literally papered with them. . . . For many days I worked through them . . . and a rough catalogue in pencil made. Then I separated the more important ones and conveyed them to the presbytery.

Then he adds:

> After a thorough examination of the owners' marks and names in the books, their history as a collection began to dawn on me . . . [beginning with] the collected books of the founder, Roger Corham and his contemporary local priests . . . [and] added to by successive priests.

In 1927, the school required urgent repairs, and although some money had been raised, Fr King sold some of the furniture that he had found and some of the books, with episcopal consent. The chief piece was a Chippendale bookcase which raised £220, a considerable sum in 1927, and an illuminated Book of Hours raised £375. Years later, as the presbytery was about to be turned into the parish centre and the new Peterhouse was nearing completion, all the archives were lodged with the County Record Office, which was delighted and had wanted to examine them for some years. The archivists catalogued all the records and put the most important of them on microfiche, making them available to researchers.[6]

Turning to a more human story: in the autumn of 1929 Fr King had a visit from a nine-year-old boy who had resolved to tell the clergy that he wanted to be a priest:

> On reaching the presbytery he [the boy] saw someone in the garden dressed in working clothes and wearing a sun hat, kneeling down tending to the flower beds. 'Can you tell me please, where I could find the parish priest?' he asked. The man looked round, got to his feet, and wiped the sweat from his brow. Looking down at the boy he took off his hat and made a deep bow, saying 'at your service, Sir'.[7]

Thirty-six years later, the gardening priest would be the retiring bishop of Portsmouth, and the young boy, Derek Worlock, would have become the priest who was to succeed him. It is said that Worlock never forgot that first meeting with his predecessor in the presbytery garden.

In 1926, Fr King was appointed a canon of the cathedral, and in 1933 Pope Pius XI appointed him domestic prelate, a monsignor, and he became vicar general of the diocese (effectively Bishop Cotter's "deputy"). Like his predecessor, Bishop Cotter did not enjoy good health towards the end of his life, and he too applied to Rome for an auxiliary. On 28 May 1938 Pope Pius XI appointed Mgr King auxiliary in Portsmouth and titular Bishop of Opus.

Mgr King was ordained bishop in St Peter's, Winchester, on 15 July 1938 (the feast of St Swithun, the ninth-century Bishop of Winchester) by Bishop Cotter assisted by Bishop Peter Amigo (Southwark) and Bishop William Brown (titular of Pella and auxiliary in Southwark). The *Portsmouth Evening News* reported that the solemn and impressive service lasted over two hours and was attended by some 200 priests as well as assorted bishops, abbots and friars. The papal mandate was read aloud, and after the epistle the litany of the saints was sung while King prostrated himself before the altar. The *Veni Creator Spiritus* was sung and the imposition of hands and the anointing with oil followed. The new bishop was presented with a bishop's staff, a gift of the parishioners, and a replica of a Cornish shepherd's crook. An episcopal ring was placed upon his finger and the book of the Gospels was placed in his hands. After the Mass, the *Te Deum* was sung and the new bishop gave his episcopal blessing for the first time. Finally, a private luncheon followed.

Two years later, in October 1940, Bishop Cotter died and Bishop King became vicar capitular and was subsequently appointed to succeed Bishop Cotter, although this was not announced until June 1941. Apparently, on the spur of the moment, he took the motto *amor vincit omnia*, meaning "love conquers everything", but it was only later that he discovered from the Benedictine nuns at St Cecilia's in Ryde that this was not a biblical quotation, as episcopal mottoes usually are, but derives from The Prologue of *The Canterbury Tales* by Chaucer. Asked about a coat of arms, he replied that a King should have a crown, and so he took one of the three crowns from the crest of his *alma mater*, Douai Abbey School.

As the new Bishop of Portsmouth, King might have been expected to move to the city, but Bishop's House was destroyed in an enemy air raid by the German *Luftwaffe* on 10 January 1941, and so Bishop King continued to live in Winchester. It is poignant to observe that if Bishop Cotter had lived just three months longer, he would most likely have died in the bombing that destroyed his house and killed the six people inside. Moreover, part of Bishop King's new diocese, the Channel Islands, became the only part of the British Isles to be occupied by the Germans during the war.

If the episcopate of William Cotter was a time of consolidation during the depression and a time of great unemployment in the 1920s and 1930s, the episcopate of Bishop King was a time of growth and expansion. The

Catholic population increased markedly from 54,000 in 1941 to 125,500 in 1965, and new Catholic parishes and schools were established too. Perhaps first and foremost were repairs to the cathedral following the 1941 bombing. In particular, all the stained glass in the building, except the Dean's Window in the south transept, was badly damaged, and this was repaired or replaced by Arthur Buss in the 1950s. The windows at the east end were redesigned and those in the clerestory were replaced by clear glass to give more light.

Bishop's House was rebuilt although Bishop King remained living in Winchester. In 1960, the rebuilding of Bishop's House in Portsmouth was complete and Bishop King might have moved to Portsmouth, but in the event the Holy See appointed Bishop Holland as his coadjutor bishop (see below). As he was a naval man, it seemed suitable to accommodate him in Portsmouth and Bishop King "stayed on in his beloved Winchester".[8]

Holland recalls that at his appointment he had never met Bishop King, but was informed (by Bishop David Cashman) that King looked "very much like God the Father, only slightly older".[9] He adds, having subsequently met the archbishop, that he had a sanguine complexion, bright eyes and a flowing beard, which he grew in later years to avoid shaving, as he suffered from eczema. Of course, he also smoked a pipe, and a photograph of him in venerable old age sees him holding his pipe in his left hand. Bishop Holland, also movingly recalled, Archbishop King "held me with a glittering eye as we smoked our pipes together in that ancient presbytery in Jewry Street".

Towards the end of the war and in the post-war period, there was great expansion in the north of the diocese. A large RAF station was established at Grove, originally as a training station, and it was later used by the American Air Force as a staging post for the planned Normandy landings. One of the huts there was a chapel where Mass was celebrated fortnightly. Bishop King blessed the chapel and on 1 December 1948 the *Sligo Champion* recorded:

> There has just been completed at Grove Camp, Wantage, Berkshire, England a beautiful little Catholic chapel and it will ever remain a monument to the Irish men who built it in their spare time . . . the little church was blessed and opened by [the]

Most Rev Dr King, Bishop of Portsmouth who congratulated the men and Mr Patrick Tansey of Kilfree, Gurteen who directed the work.

A prisoner-of-war camp was established between Wantage and East Challow, now in Oxfordshire; and in Wantage, Didcot and Abingdon the population grew, especially as employment opportunities expanded. In 1946, the Atomic Energy Research Establishment was formed and opened at RAF Harwell, just outside Wantage, and the population generally, and the Catholic population in particular, expanded rapidly. The site, known affectionately at the time as "the Atomic", became one of the main employers in the post-war period, with many imported workers replacing the pre-war predominantly agrarian economy.

As a result of this considerable expansion of the population in the area, Bishop King decided that Wantage needed its own priest. He wrote in his Rosary Sunday letter of 1947: "Already a large influx of Catholics has taken place, so that it has become necessary to establish a priest at Wantage." It is said that when the new Irish priest, Fr Daniel Cogan, arrived in Wantage there were 1,000 people waiting for him. In July 1952, Bishop King travelled to Wantage and confirmed 17 children and 15 adult converts. This was the first confirmation in Wantage since the Reformation. Again, in his Rosary Sunday letter of 1947, Bishop King wrote, "To sum up, there are now nine priests in this area: Mass is said each Sunday at thirteen different places and the total Catholic population must be within sight of 5,000."[10]

There were new parishes and churches on the islands in the diocese too. In June 1947, a new church dedicated to the Sacred Heart was consecrated and opened at St Aubin on Jersey. In 1952, a new church dedicated to St David was opened at East Cowes on the Isle of Wight, the previous church there having been completely destroyed during a bombing raid in 1942. St Saviour's Church in Totland on the Isle of Wight was opened by Bishop Cotter in 1923, but not consecrated until all the debts had been paid in May 1954. On this occasion, Bishop King presided, tracing the Latin and Greek alphabets across the surface of the walls, to show the consecration extended to the whole building. Twelve crosses on the inner walls were anointed with the oil of chrism.

Bembridge, on the Isle of Wight, expanded rapidly in the 1950s and many new houses were built. Although there had been provision for Catholics in a former Wesleyan chapel, it was not until 1965 that a new purpose-built church was opened there. In June 1959, Archbishop King had visited Ryde to administer confirmation. He made a private visit to Bembridge with the parish priest Fr Daniel Cogan (no longer in Wantage), and the two men agreed a modern Catholic church for the village was a priority. The architect C. A. F. Sheppard of Ryde, who had designed Holy Cross in Seaview, was commissioned to make plans for the new church, which was built and finally opened on the second Sunday after Pentecost 1965. Lacking the ornament of St Mary's Church in Ryde, it has been described as serene and beautiful, employing a harmony of colours and natural light.

Another notably beautiful church of the period was the most northerly parish church in the diocese: Holy Rood Church, just south of Oxford. Described as "a landmark in English Catholic Ecclesiology", it was inspired by Maguire and Murray's St Paul's Church, Bow Common. Designed by Gilbert Flavel, its octagonal design set within a Greek cross, is sympathetic to the new post-conciliar liturgical thinking. The internal furnishings in the sanctuary (including the *corona lucis* above the altar) and in the Blessed Sacrament chapel are remarkable too. It was built at a cost of £35,000 and dedicated by Bishop Holland (King's auxiliary) on 16 December 1961.

In 1967, the Catholic newspaper *The Universe* published a supplement listing all 25 of the new churches built and opened in the diocese. Of course, Bishop King cannot claim responsibility for each and every one, but he certainly created an ethos of optimism and opportunity amongst his clergy and his people.

Following the Butler Act in 1944, there was an increase in the number of Catholic schools too. The act allowed for the establishment of Voluntary Aided Schools. In this arrangement, the state funded all the running costs of the school, but the foundation—in this case the Catholic Church—met some of the capital costs in exchange for a greater influence of the admission, policies, staffing and curriculum of the school. In some dioceses, these costs were met by a central diocesan fund, but Bishop King left it to the priests of each deanery to raise the funds. A huge programme of fundraising was undertaken: "Voluntary subscriptions, bank loans, football pools, garden fetes, bazaars ... [and] as the records show his [Bishop King's] priests did not fail him."[11] Many Catholic primary and secondary schools were established.

One in particular is perhaps worthy of note: Archbishop King Middle School in Carisbrooke, near Newport on the Isle of Wight. This was a well-respected voluntary-aided Catholic school founded in 1974 and known locally as "ABK". In 2008, the school merged with the nearby Church of England Trinity School to form the joint Catholic / Church of England secondary school and sixth-form college called Christ the King.

In 1950, Bishop King's life path intersected with another future archbishop in an interesting way. Cormac Murphy-O'Connor, recognizing a call to priesthood, and in his own words being attracted to London, "the bright lights and the big city",[12] resolved to apply to the Westminster Archdiocese rather than his home diocese of Portsmouth. Murphy-O'Connor's father spoke to Bishop King, who refused to permit him to apply to Westminster, keeping him for Portsmouth. This meant that for one year only there were three Murphy-O'Connor brothers all studying at the Venerable English College in Rome together. In an amusing twist—and it is often said God must have a sense of humour—Murphy-O'Connor did join the Archdiocese of Westminster, not as a priest, but as Archbishop in March 2000.

In 1953, Bishop King set up his own Diocesan Child Welfare Society with Fr Francis Phillips as the first administrator. This was essentially an adoption service, and some 600 babies were adopted or fostered by Catholic families. Later legislation rather changed this aspect of Catholic welfare work, and the Diocesan Welfare Society closed in 1968. Archbishop King's successor, Bishop Worlock, introduced a new provision, but this proved very costly for one diocese and the provision merged with similar organizations in the Archdiocese of Southwark and the Diocese of Arundel and Brighton.

In 1954, Bishop King celebrated 50 years as a priest and was appointed Archbishop *ad personam* by Pope Pius XII. To be clear, this was a personal honour and did not make Portsmouth an archdiocese, nor King a metropolitan archbishop. Additionally, in 1954, Bishop King met HM Queen Elizabeth II at Windsor on the occasion of the St George's

Day Guides' parade. Ten years later, when he celebrated the diamond jubilee of his ordination, Bishop Holland tells us King had little idea of the affection and esteem in which he was held by clergy and laity alike. However, he was moved by the "boys and girls of the diocese who gathered round him with little more than their love and their joy plus an illuminated scroll assuring him of both".[13]

In November 1958, Archbishop King gave his approval for the opening of an Opus Dei house in Oxford. This is worth mentioning, since there is an erroneous story that Archbishop George Dwyer, of Birmingham Archdiocese, opposed the establishment of an Opus Dei house in his territory, and so Grandpont House, just south of the River Thames and therefore in the "more compliant" Diocese of Portsmouth, was acquired instead. William O'Connor has shown that this narrative is not consonant with the facts, since Grandpont House was bought by Opus Dei in July 1959 and Archbishop Dwyer was not translated to Birmingham (from Leeds) until 1965.

Netherhall House, an Opus Dei house in London, was opened in 1952, and on a visit there in 1958 Mgr, now Saint, Josemaría Escrivá, the founder of Opus Dei, suggested that student residences might be established in other university cities, including Oxford:

> On 19 November 1958 Bishop King of Portsmouth was asked for permission for the setting up of a centre of Opus Dei in his part of Oxford and also for an appointment to see him. On 21 November Bishop King gladly granted his permission.[14]

It is worth noting that Grandpont House in Oxford remains an Opus Dei house, serving members of the University of Oxford, and others, to this day.

In 1962, Pope John XXIII convened the Second Vatican Council. Unlike many of the previous Councils, this was not designed to clarify or update Church doctrine, but was famously convened in a spirit of *aggiornamento*—to open the windows [of the Church] and let in some fresh air. The aim of the Council was to bring the Church up to date: to review its relationship with, and mission to, the world. More recently, the late emeritus Pope Benedict XVI affirmed that the most important message of the Council is "the Paschal mystery at the centre of what it is to be Christian and therefore of the Christian life, the Christian year, the Christian seasons".[15] The council was formally opened on 11 October 1962 and had 11 commissions and three secretariats, which would finally produce four constitutions, three declarations and nine decrees.

Having said this, Archbishop King was excused from attending the council on account of his age (he was 82), although he watched what he could on the television. While the council was in session, he was the only bishop remaining in England. Midway through the council, in 1963, Archbishop King celebrated the silver jubilee of his episcopal ordination, and the priests and people of the diocese gave him a handsome cheque which he donated towards the training of clergy for the diocese.

Archbishop King wrote about the council's proposed changes to the Mass in the 1965 Diocesan Directory, emphasizing that we gather at Mass as a family, and this is underlined by our "common prayer—our praying aloud together"[16] and, of course, predominantly in English. In the 1970 *Year Book*, a longer article by the Very Revd W. R. Lawrence entitled "The New Order of the Mass" and reproduced from the Redemptorists' weekly bulletin, *Christian Encounter*, was included. It emphasized that the new rite of the Mass should lead priest and people into deeper understanding and fuller participation. Nobody could argue with that but it also highlighted that the new rite was much more flexible, allowing some elements of the rite to be included or not, said or sung, embellished or simplified as circumstances dictate.[17] This understanding marked a significant new approach to liturgical celebration. The new rite was finally promulgated by Pope Paul VI in 1969 and introduced into the liturgy in 1970.

After living in the presbytery in Winchester for almost 40 years, Archbishop King was admitted to a Winchester nursing home in March 1965 and died a few days later (perhaps surprisingly still in office) on 23 March 1965 (aged 84). The *Portsmouth Evening News* reported his death the following day, adding that he would be remembered for his wisdom and sincerity, his dignity and simplicity, and his humanity. The report added: "He will be recalled by thousands of Catholics in his vast diocese for his naturalness, gaiety and chuckling good humour which punctuated his conversation and his speeches."

His body lay in state in the Lady Chapel of St Peter's, Winchester, until his Requiem Mass was celebrated there, on 19 March, by Cardinal John Heenan, Archbishop of Westminster. Mgr Sidney Mullarkey (vicar capitular for the diocese) was the assistant priest and Provost Bernard Lindsay and Canon Robert Scantlebury carried out the deacon's duties.

The Mass was celebrated in Latin with priests from the diocese and students from De La Salle College singing a plainsong requiem. Mgr Mullarkey preached the homily. The final absolutions were given by five prelates and the music for the absolutions was composed by a priest of the diocese, Mgr John Crookhall (*d*.1887); it had first been used at the funeral of Cardinal Wiseman in 1865.

Immediately after the requiem, Archbishop King was buried in St James' Cemetery, Winchester, again by Mgr Mullarkey. In medieval times, a church dedicated to St James and a graveyard occupied the site, but after the plague the parish ceased to exist and the church was eventually demolished. However, the cemetery remained and has been used for the exclusive burial of Catholics ever since. Most of the parish priests of St Peter's are buried there, as well as nuns, French refugee priests and members of the nobility and humbler folk. Archbishop King's own parents are buried there (and Bishop Worlock's too), and it is where, it is said, Bishop King spent many happy hours deciphering tombstones, and recording his findings in his "Sermons in Stone": describing the burial ground in which lie so many of our illustrious dead. He once wrote: "This sacred spot, epitome of the penal days, the first tangible and material mark of unity which the Catholics of Hampshire possessed, a rallying point for the scattered Catholics of the shire."

Archbishop King's own plot is just inside the entrance gate. His tombstone is a pentagonal prism on the end of which is his episcopal coat of arms. One of the upper faces bears, in stone, an episcopal crozier and the other bears the simple inscription:

JOHN HENRY KING + ARCHBISHOP

16 IX 1880—23 III 1965

BISHOP OF PORTSMOUTH + REQUIESCAT IN PACE

During his long life, Archbishop King never learnt to drive a car; he never entered a cinema or attended a sporting event. He had simple tastes in food, preferring raw onion and cold meats to cooked dishes, but it is said that, on account of his Italian seminary formation, he was partial to a glass of red wine.

Notes

1   *British Journal of Educational Studies* 24:1 (February 1976), p. 33.

2   Gerard Dwyer, *Diocese of Portsmouth: Past and Present* (Portsmouth: Portsmouth Diocesan Centenary Committee, 1981), p. 104.

3   Cf. Michael Williams, *The Venerable English College, Rome* (Leominster: Gracewing, 1979, 2008), p. 184.

4   Dwyer, *Diocese of Portsmouth: Past and Present*, p. 104.

5   Cf. *St Peter's Catholic Church Winchester* by John Thornhill and Sue Broadbent (2019).

6   Cf. *Catholic Archives* 1990 (no 10), pp. 7ff., an article by Peter Paul Bogan.

7   John Furnival and Ann Knowles, *Archbishop Derek Worlock: His Personal Journey* (London: Geoffrey Chapman, 1998), p. 1.

8   Ibid., p. 115.

9   Thomas Holland, *For Better and for Worse* (Salford: Salford Diocese, 1989), p. 196.

10   Quoted in Dwyer, *Diocese of Portsmouth: Past and Present*, p. 106.

11   Dwyer, *Diocese of Portsmouth: Past and Present*, p. 111.

12   Cormac Murphy-O'Connor, *An English Spring* (London: Bloomsbury, 2015), p. 26.

13   Holland, *For Better and for Worse*, p. 211.

14   William O'Connor, *Opus Dei: An Open Book* (Dublin: The Mercier Press, 1991), p. 144.

15   Meeting with the Parish Priests and Clergy of Rome Diocese, 14 February 2013.

16   1965 *Diocesan Year Book*, p. 162.

17   Cf. 1970 *Diocesan Year Book*, p. 139.

4 A

Thomas Holland (1961–63)

Thomas Holland was born in Southport, Lancashire on 11 June 1908, to John Holland and his wife Mary (née Fletcher). He was one of seven children and was baptized in the local Church of the Holy Family by the parish priest, Father George Richmond. As a young child, he travelled by tram, two miles each way into town, to be educated by the Selly Park Sisters at St Marie's Catholic School where, first and foremost, the catechism was drilled into him.

Aged 12, in 1920, young Thomas joined the junior seminary, St Joseph's College at Upholland, near Wigan, as his elder brother had done. Regrettably no more (Upholland closed as a seminary in 1987 and the buildings were sold by the diocese in 1996), it was founded in 1880 by Bishop Bernard O'Reilly to be a seminary for northwest England, and in particular for the diocese of Liverpool. The college was "an ample, and in parts handsome, sandstone building in wide grounds with two lakes and extensive farm and orchards".[1] At its height, there was a junior seminary for schoolboys and a major seminary preparing men for ordination— some 200 boys and men in total.

Sir Anthony Kenny, who was a pupil at the junior seminary there (albeit some 30 years after Holland) gives us something of the liturgical flavour (which had probably not changed much) as he recalls:

> The offices of Holy Week and of Christmas were the climax of the year at Upholland. The Christmas Office lasted from 10pm on Christmas Eve until about 2am: first the Christmas Matins (nine psalms, lessons and antiphons), then the Midnight Mass, and immediately afterwards the Christmas Lauds (five psalms, a hymn and a canticle) . . . But for overall dramatic effect the

Christmas Office was far outdone by the ceremonies of Holy Week. The entire week before Easter Sunday was given over to religious observances.[2]

A retreat took place in the first part of Holy Week. The elaborate services of the triduum were performed with great precision, following careful rehearsal.

Amongst other things, Holland played cricket and in an extant photograph of the Upholland XI, he is noted as the wicket-keeper. At the end of the following academic year, Holland was summoned to see the vice-rector, Dr Richard Downey (later Archbishop of Liverpool), who told him he was to be transferred to the English College in Valladolid. In what seems a rather brutal remark to me but was probably par for the course at the time, Downey apparently said, "When plants fail to come to their best in one soil ... nurserymen move them. You are to be transplanted to the English College in Spain."[3]

And so it was, that after seven years at Upholland, at the end of the summer holidays in September 1927, seminarian Thomas Holland found himself on a train from London Victoria, via Dover to Paris (where he spent two days), and then onward through western France to Spain. On board, he met others bound for the English College, including Fr C. C. Martindale SJ, who was to give the retreat at the beginning of that academic year.

St Alban's English College in Valladolid was originally founded in the late sixteenth century to train priests for the English Mission. Among its alumni, the college can boast of some six saints and 17 *beati* (most of whom were beatified by Pope John Paul II on 22 November 1987). After an initial year, Holland studied philosophy at the *Universidad Pontificia* ("the Pont") in Valladolid. He recalls: "Cassocked, caped, shovel-hatted and in crocodile, seven second year philosophers left the College at 8.40 for Don Mariano's first lecture of the 1927–28 academic year ... in the Calle Cardinal Sanz y Fores."[4] Cosmology and physics were also on the syllabus alongside sacred scripture, fundamental theology, Latin, Hebrew and moral philosophy:

You came to know Spain and the Spaniards, as you wandered on
donkeys, bikes, buses, shanks' pony. Perhaps best of all there was
a chance simply to sit back and drink in the long views across
the pine forests and the cornfields rolling away to the flat-topped
hills. Even now when I think of heaven, distraction will crowd
in of a certain clump of pines above our Country House, a
deck-chair, a pipe, a book and the long view to Simancas Castle
nestling above the River Pisuerga.[5]

After six years in Spain, Holland was ordained priest for the Archdiocese
of Liverpool by Archbishop Richard Downey, back in St Marie's Church,
Southport on 18 June 1933. This was the church where Holland had made
his first confession, his first holy communion, and where he had been
confirmed by Archbishop Thomas Whiteside. Following his ordination
to the priesthood, he celebrated his first Mass there on 19 June 1933. After
this, the young Fr Holland then spent three months assisting at Sacred
Heart Church, Hall Lane in Liverpool. It was here that he came across a
man who showed him a creased paper written in Latin and dated 1917,
confirming that he had been given basic instruction in the faith, been
baptized and received his first holy communion *imminente praelio*—on
the eve of battle. Holland would do something similar himself in the
Second World War. This spell at Sacred Heart was also significant, for
it was the only time in his life that he actually served in the diocese for
which he had been ordained.

After this brief spell in a parish, and as he subsequently discovered,
with Rector Henson (at Valladolid) pulling strings in the background, the
young Fr Holland was sent to Rome to study for his doctorate. He was
enrolled at the English Beda College, for more mature students, and at
the Gregorian University. He studied the full range of theology courses
and additional courses in scripture, canon law and pastoral theology.

After two years, Fr Holland had completed the daunting array of
theological studies and examinations and spent his third year writing his
thesis on pneumatology (the study of the Holy Spirit), and in particular on
the action of the Holy Spirit outside the Church. The title of his thesis was
The Holy Spirit and the Anglo-Catholic Movement. Fr Holland worked to
the wire, picking up the last typed sections the day before the submission

deadline. However, these pages had not been bound and Holland had to take recourse to a paper merchant working late in the cellars of the Beda, who bound the copies of his thesis in grey sugar-bag paper.

When he came to submit the thesis the following day at the Gregorian, the clerk at the office announced, "It won't stand up," a damning judgement of the new *magnum opus*. What he meant was that the bound text could not stand in the vertical position. Fr Holland looked the clerk firmly in the eye and slipped him 5 lire, and the clerk said "*Eh, eh, proviamo.*" meaning "Okay, we'll give it a go!" In time, Fr Holland successfully defended his thesis, gave the mandatory specimen theology lecture to a near-empty lecture hall and had, in effect, completed his STD: his Doctorate in Sacred Theology. In actual fact, it was not formally awarded until some nine years later, when as is, or was, the continental custom, a version of the thesis had been published.

Alongside his studies, Fr Holland's spiritual life was deepened and developed by a weekly visit

> to the Beda from the Black Pope's HQ, the *Casa Generalizia* of the Jesuits. Promptly at 11.45 every Friday, Fr Joe Welsby began his spiritual conference, always finishing as the clock struck 12 noon for the Angelus, after which we filed in for lunch. There was a gemlike quality about the man and his words. In conferences or confession they were clear, spare, hard but never harsh.[6]

In addition to study, he also got to know Rome very well, leaving the Beda College most days by 6 a.m. to celebrate Mass in the basilicas and churches of Rome. He and his companions also made excursions beyond Rome during holidays and *exeats*, to Assisi, Perugia, Todi and elsewhere.

After his three years in Rome, Holland was sent back to the English College in Valladolid between 1936 and 1942, under the rector Fr Edwin Henson. The vice-rector, Father James Turner, and Fr Holland did most of the teaching: four lectures each morning five days a week. The vice-rector lectured in sacred scripture, morals, dogmatics and ethics, while Holland taught logic, metaphysics, cosmology and allied disciplines.

In addition to his theological teaching, he and all the residents at the English College in Valladolid had to cope with the Spanish Civil War which broke out the evening before Fr Holland travelled to Spain (in 1936) and lasted until April 1939. Here is not the place for a discussion of that conflict. Just six months later, the outbreak of the Second World War and Britain's entry into it in September 1939, put the lives of English Catholics in Spain into some jeopardy. In his report to the English bishops in 1941, the rector spoke of rationing, and in a subsequent letter to Fr John Petit (later Bishop of Menevia), he wrote that the country was on the verge of starvation. The Scots College at Valladolid and the Irish College at Salamanca were both closed.

In 1940, the idea of moving the few remaining English students in Spain to Lisbon in Portugal (which was neutral in the Second World War) was considered. Early in 1942, the Bishop of Northampton (Thomas Parker) decided to recall the vice-rector, Fr Hardwicke, and his students, who were ready to be ordained, returned to England too. Additionally, the rector of the English College in Lisbon was about to have major surgery, and so Fr Holland was asked to stand in for him and to take along the seven remaining Valladolid students. They were too few to maintain real college life in Valladolid, and so they were transferred, along with their new temporary rector, to Lisbon to complete their clerical studies there. Rector Henson was left behind alone in his college at Valladolid.

Unfortunately, the rector of the English College in Lisbon, Mgr John Cullen, having originally recovered well from his surgery, took a turn for the worse and died in the summer. So it fell to Fr Holland to maintain the routine of seminary life. In the summer that year, Holland made a pilgrimage on foot to Fatima which was personally blessed by the Archbishop of Mitylene, the vicar general of the Patriarch of Lisbon.

The following academic year, Fr Holland took over the late rector's teaching duties and a number of other pastoral opportunities opened up: days of recollection for the British community, catechism in the English school at Carcavellos, saying Mass at an enclosed Portuguese convent—even the odd sermon in Portuguese.

There was a lively social round in Lisbon, and on a visit to Porto, Fr Holland was the guest of Ron Symmington, of Symmington port fame. Additionally, guests regularly arrived at the professors' table in Lisbon en route to or from Rome. But Fr Holland was not to remain in Portugal, and a new rector was appointed for the following academic year. Holland ended his relatively brief sojourn at the English College in Lisbon in the summer of 1943 and was granted honorary life membership of the Lisbonian Society for alumni.

After his time in Lisbon and with the permission and blessing of Archbishop Downey, between 1944 and 1946 Fr Holland volunteered as a chaplain in the Royal Navy, completing his basic training at the Royal Marines Small Arms Training Camp at Dalditch near Exeter. Later, Holland was decorated for his work as a chaplain, earning the DSC (Distinguished Service Cross) for conspicuous bravery. The citation stated the award was conferred for gallantry, skill, determination and undaunted devotion to duty during the landing of the Allied Forces on the coast of Normandy. An article by Mgr John Allen, which appears on the Salford Diocese website, is worth quoting at some length, because it gives us a fascinating insight into Holland's character:

> His ship was the *Ascanius*, fittingly enough registered in Liverpool, with a mainly Liverpudlian crew. Bishop Holland recalled how he had a neat but tidy cabin but then as we hit the Normandy beaches I surrendered my cabin to our first casualty. I'd little choice, in fact. Even so, I remember being vividly overwhelmed by the ecstasy of possessing nothing—an unmerited Franciscan thrill of joy.
>
> He recalled the boom of the guns as their ship neared the shore and the splash of the shells all round them from German fire. Arriving on the coast he moved from ship to ship between Juno and Sword and Gold Beaches. There were many casualties from high fragmentation shells and he had a lot to do. [On] one vessel he boarded . . . a shell had pierced the ratings' mess room. The only living creature to emerge unscathed was the ship's dog. That night he had a tent ashore. I remember bedding down . . . too tired to bother about whether I'd be there in the morning.
>
> As the days passed he spent many a night on the last ship he visited. He was the only Catholic chaplain in the area and consequently his services were much in demand. He would celebrate Mass each day for whatever crew members were able to attend and he encouraged the men to avail themselves

of confession. On one ship he baptized more than two dozen
Congolese sailors giving them minimum instruction in the faith,
christening them all with the name Peter, and giving them a
certificate to show to the priest in the Congo when they got home.

Fr Holland also spent time as a chaplain in Rouen, Lisieux and at Antwerp
in Belgium, and after a spell of leave in the summer of 1946 he was given
the instruction, "Sail on M. V. Strathnever for duty as R.C. Chaplain on
H.M.S. Lanka, Ceylon."[7] HMS *Lanka*, it should be noted, was not a ship,
but a complex of onshore establishments, including a college, a military
hospital and a rest camp. Tropical kit, including white shorts, was
issued and Holland travelled to St Philip Neri's church in Pettah, where
he would be based for the next 12 months, working alongside a priest
of the Missionary Order of Mary Immaculate (OMI). His main tasks
were celebrating the Mass, administering the sacraments and providing
pastoral support. At Christmas Midnight Mass in 1945, Holland found
himself singing the carol *See amid the winter snow* in the tropics!

At the end of the war, the naval presence in Ceylon began to be
dismantled and Holland received word from Archbishop Roberts
of Bombay that HMS *Lanka*'s days were numbered. The archbishop
suggested that rather than return home "mission accomplished", would
he consider acting as a port chaplain in one of the many ports that were
opening up again to civilian traffic? Holland agreed to the proposal and
was sent to Bombay (now Mumbai), taking up residence in the cathedral
clergy house with ten other clerics, including the former cathedral
administrator, Fr Gracias, who had been appointed auxiliary bishop,
and who would go on to become the first Indian cardinal.

Holland concentrated his activities at the port, centred on the Heart
and Anchor Club on Ballard Pier, which had a chapel, a library and other
amenities. The heart and anchor is the emblem of the Apostleship of
the Sea, now known as *Stella Maris*. Holland's day-to-day work was the
maritime equivalent of house visiting, going from ship to ship along the
quays. After a while, Holland stood in for a Jesuit priest and ran a parish
too at Colaba Point, where Holland was provided with a bungalow, a
push bike, two servants and the Jesuit's cat.

On Christmas Day 1946, Holland was officially demobbed from the Navy and became a civilian chaplain. He continued in Bombay before a final spell as port chaplain in Calcutta (now Kolkata). In mid-1948, he returned to England, and there was a suggestion that he might go and work with the new Bishop of Menevia (John Petit), who intended to found a Catholic Missionary Society in Wales. After some discussions, Holland's archbishop decided against this idea but sent him to join the Catholic Missionary Society in London, where he remained until 1956, spending his last five years there as editor of the *Catholic Gazette*, the society's journal.

The CMS was established in 1901 by Cardinal Vaughan, Archbishop of Westminster, to be an organization for mission at home, alongside the Mill Hill Society, which he also founded for mission overseas. The particular apostolate of CMS was "to bring back the faith to England and Wales by means of sermons in churches and public lectures in halls".[8] The *Catholic Gazette* was first published in 1910.

The CMS house at Brondesbury had been destroyed in a bombing raid during the war, and in their Low Week meeting the bishops had discussed whether to let the CMS die or attempt to revive it. The majority of bishops were in favour of letting it fade away, but the Apostolic Delegate, Archbishop William Godfrey, warned that such a failure in the spirit of evangelization would not look good in Rome. In 1947, the bishops appointed Fr John Heenan as the new superior of CMS, succeeding Fr Owen Dudley (who had been superior since 1933), and a revitalization was underway. Heenan went off to America to study how similar organizations worked across the Atlantic, and on his return, he founded a new house in West Heath Road, Hampstead. Four new members took up residence at the house in Hampstead in November 1947, and "Fathers Callaghan and Holland soon joined from Liverpool and Fr Martindale came from Lancaster".[9]

Holland's work for CMS took him across the country, and at Heenan's suggestion the work of the Mission was extended not only to all parishes in England and Wales but to HM Prisons too. Holland visited Wormwood Scrubs as well as prisons in Lincoln and Birmingham. In early 1951, Heenan became Bishop of Leeds and Fr George Dwyer was appointed to succeed him as superior of CMS. Change followed quite quickly with a number of new recruits to CMS and Holland replacing Dwyer as editor of the *Catholic Gazette*. In Holland's own words, there was a brilliant team of contributors, notably Frs Gerald Culkin, History Professor and Chris Maguire, Science Professor from Ushaw; and Fr Alec Jones, Scripture Professor at Upholland. Overall, Holland has described his time with CMS in the most positive of terms, relishing the theological teamwork and the shared merriment.

Holland's last mission was a six-month trip to New Zealand with Fr George Dwyer at the request of the bishops of New Zealand. Holland wrote that there was never a dull moment and described the country as: "Fjords of Norway, mountains of Wales, glaciers of Switzerland, gold of the Klondykes, stags of the Grampians, lakes of Canada and no place more than forty miles from two great oceans fringed with golden beaches, teeming with fish."[10]

Holland recalls bathing in hot springs at Rotorua and enjoying ham for supper which had been baked by inserting it in a hole in the presbytery garden! They also preached and taught in cathedrals and churches, universities and schools, retreat houses, and on the radio too. In the main, Holland and Dwyer acted independently, but they joined together for university debates and school retreats. Furthermore, in New Zealand, the life of a priest was more than integrated with "everyday life", and Holland recalls helping to move herds of sheep and burying a Māori girl, not to mention the routine preaching, all of which would eventually lead to a temporary loss of voice for the loquacious missioner. Holland also preached and broadcast at Invercargill, the nearest city to the South Pole, and on Fiji too.

It was while he was in New Zealand that he received a letter from the Apostolic Delegate in London, Archbishop Gerald O'Hara, inviting him to be O'Hara's personal secretary. Holland replied that he was unable to accept because of a long commitment in New Zealand. There was a further reply that he would be expected by the Apostolic Delegate when the New Zealand trip was completed. Holland travelled home from New Zealand via the United States, and he remarks that flying into San Francisco early in the morning, never had he seen an earthly city so beautiful:

The sun rose behind it as we approached, endowing spires, domes, tower block with a radiant sharpness one associates with Grecian cities of Parian marble famed by poets for just that unearthly splendour.[11]

Archbishop Gerald O'Hara (1895–1963) was an American who had served as a bishop in America before entering the Vatican diplomatic service in 1947. In 1954, he was appointed Apostolic Delegate to Great Britain, Malta, Gibraltar and Bermuda. In 1960, O'Hara made a historic visit to the Houses of Parliament; indeed he was the first papal representative to do so in more than 400 years. He died of a heart attack in Wimbledon in 1963.

Holland presented himself at the Apostolic Delegation at Parkside, in Wimbledon, southwest London, on 17 December 1956, as successor to David Cashman who would go on to be the first Bishop of Arundel and Brighton. Holland was promoted to the rank of Monsignor and was part of a team of a dozen or so, working for the archbishop at the Delegation. There were four Sisters of the Medical Missionaries of Mary, two Irish house maids, His Excellency's man-servant Buss from America, a typist, a resident canon lawyer, Fr Joe Jones CSSR, a counsellor, a driver (Morty), and a gardener with whom Holland modestly, if not tongue-in-cheek, described himself as bringing up the rear.

Mgr Holland's main duties were managing O'Hara's diary and schedule, coordinating the many events and receptions to which he was invited and organizing guest lists and details for reciprocal hospitality. Holland was also involved in communications with the Vatican and assisting with the process of selecting new candidates to be bishops— whilst sworn to secrecy, of course.

Additionally, Holland accompanied O'Hara on his travels to Scotland and to Wales and in 1960 to Malta (which was under the responsibility of the London Delegation) for the nineteenth centenary of St Paul's shipwreck there. Also in 1960, which Holland has described as his *Annus Mirabilis*, they travelled to the 37th International Eucharistic Congress in Munich.

Later that year, Mgr Holland was taking some holiday and travelling in Britain when he himself received the telephone call from the Delegation.

It was on 28 October, when Holland was giving a day of recollection to the priests belonging to the Society of the Little Flower at the Sisters of Charity Convent in Carlisle Place, that the telephone call came from Archbishop O'Hara. Owing to the formal nature of the request, the Delegate asked (in Latin) if he would accept the pope's decision, to which he replied "*libenter*", "willingly". Although to be kept secret until the official announcement, O'Hara gave his permission for the news to be shared at the convent and "further reading of the *History of a Soul* was suspended and wine was called for".[12]

Holland was officially appointed titular Bishop of *Etenna* and coadjutor Bishop of Portsmouth by Pope Saint John XXIII, on 31 October 1960. He left the Apostolic Delegation on 17 December 1960, four years to the day after he had arrived, and just four days later, he was ordained bishop in the Cathedral of St John, Portsmouth on 21 December 1960. The principal consecrator was Archbishop John King (Portsmouth) assisted by Bishop George Dwyer (Bishop of Leeds and later Archbishop of Birmingham) and Bishop John Healy (Gibraltar). Unbeknown to him, there had been some "discussion" behind the scenes as Archbishop O'Hara, his former boss, had wanted to ordain him, as had Cardinal William Godfrey, the Metropolitan Archbishop of Westminster, the province in which Portsmouth lay at the time.

Bishop Holland recalls that after the ceremony he took some time to divest in the sacristy, struggling with the full episcopal panoply for the first time. By the time he reached the bishop's house, it was silent, all the others having already left for the reception in Southsea:

> Outside, Edinburgh Road was innocent of all transport. I stood helpless . . . A milk-van appeared. It was grossly unfair but I pleaded a lift. Time was running out on me. He opened his door. More, he pronounced himself honoured. We made the South Beach Hotel in record time.[13]

The new bishop took up residence in Bishop's House in Portsmouth, while Archbishop King remained living in Winchester. The administration of the cathedral and bishop's house were in the capable hands of Fr T. Dwyer and his housekeeper, Miss Norah. Travelling around the diocese, the new bishop could be assured of a square meal on his return home, and on "chapter days", the canons' lunch did honour to the house. When Fr Dwyer, and particularly Miss Norah, moved on to a vacant parish, the domestic arrangements in Bishop's House rather deteriorated, until they were rescued by the arrival of four sisters from the Franciscan Missionaries of St Joseph (FMSJ Sisters).

But the move to Portsmouth, the "Home of the Royal Navy", was undoubtedly propitious for Bishop Holland, and the Royal Navy was kind to the new boy. The Admiral in Command of the dockyard invited him to dine on the *Victory* in Nelson's day cabin, and when a Spanish sailing and training ship, the *Sagres*, called into Portsmouth, Holland was invited to visit. He was especially requested not to show up in civvies, as the American prelates had done, but to wear everything that went with his rank.

Cardinal Cormac Murphy-O'Connor observed later: "The idea was that he [Bishop Holland] would soon take over the reins, but King rather woke up again at Tommy's appearance and didn't let him do anything really. He was told to go round the diocese visiting all the convents. It was frustrating for him."[14] Gerard Dwyer put a slightly more positive spin on the matter: "Bishop Holland worked in the diocese for four years, encouraging vocations, promoting new schools and catechetics, conducting visitations and administering the Sacrament of Confirmation. He became well known and well liked by priests and religious people."[15]

Holland recalls that piece by piece, a large mosaic began to form of priests and parishes, brothers and institutions, sisters, convents, schools and children. He "mugged-up" on the relevant aspects of canon law, and he began to get the "feel" of the Catholic Church in Hampshire, Berkshire, the Isle of Wight and the Channel Islands. Bishop Holland himself seemed to take especial delight in visiting the islands in the diocese. He first visited the Isle of Wight on a CMS mission in 1954, for celebrations of the Marian Year, but he clearly enjoyed subsequent visits across the Solent. He got to know Quarr Abbey well, where he went for his retreats, guided by Dom Joseph Warrilow. He became familiar with Abbot Tissot and made visits to St Cecilia's Abbey, attending various professions.

Bishop Holland also enjoyed his visits to the Channel Islands by plane, and recalls that working with the Apostolic Delegate he had come to be familiar with receptions at airports, but found it a little strange to be the one for whom the reception was arranged. He observed: "There was no great man behind whom I could trail."

Some years later in his first pastoral letter to his new diocese of Salford, he revealed quite a lot about his own feelings about his time in Portsmouth:

> Naturally I feel sad at leaving Archbishop King of Portsmouth whose assistant I have been for the last four years. He will be sixty years a priest in November if God spares him. Say a prayer for him. He is really a character ... his diocese is a beauty: Hampshire, Berkshire, Isle of Wight and the Channel Islands. You would have to be made of stone to leave such a diocese without a pang of regret, especially after receiving the kindness I have known from priests and people and from other religious bodies and civic authorities.[16]

In less than two years after his ordination to the episcopate, Bishop Holland was called to the Second Vatican Council. He attended all four sessions of the council, but at the first two sessions, presided over by Pope John XXIII, he attended as an auxiliary: he was not an official Council Father and he did not have a vote. Bishop Holland was a full Council Father at the third and fourth sessions, presided over by Pope Paul VI. Additionally, we can imagine that he would have worked very closely with the other English Council Fathers, particularly Archbishop Heenan, whom Holland knew well from CMS days.

Before the Council officially opened, Bishop Holland was nominated to Cardinal Bea's Secretariate for the Promotion of Christian Unity, with which he would be connected for 15 years in total, and he started to make contacts in the other Christian churches. He got to know Bishop John Phillips, the Anglican Bishop of Portsmouth, and his soon-to-be opposite number in the north, Bishop William ("Billy") Greer of Manchester. He also had to make increasingly frequent trips to Rome for preparatory meetings, and he stayed, while there, at the Venerable English College.

After the council, Holland's work with other churches would continue by implementing its Decree on Ecumenism, and he also became involved in the World Council of Churches (WCC). Various committee groups met regularly, and they discussed

> practical collaboration in the fields of philanthropy, social and international affairs; theological study programmes which have a specific bearing on ecumenical relations; problems which cause tension between the churches such as mixed marriages, religious liberty and proselytism, and common concerns with regard to the life of the Church such as laity, missions.[17]

Bishop Holland would later observe that the reams of paperwork associated with these ecumenical meetings were a challenge when placed alongside the responsibilities of running a diocese.

For such a young bishop—young in bishop's orders that is—Holland would make a significant and influential contribution to the council. In his book *My Journal of the Council*, Yves Congar noted that in October 1963 they were discussing *De S Liturgia* and

> Mgr Holland (England) in the name of the Bishops of England and Wales said that collegiality must be made concrete and made manifest by making the bishops co-operate in the government of the universal Church by setting up a means by which the spirit of the Council, and even in some way its reality, will be continued.[18]

To put this another way, he was one of the first bishops to call, from the council floor, for what would later be established as the Synod of Bishops. Before the Second Vatican Council, the prevailing view of the Church, and the one taught in seminaries, was a decidedly top-down model. The pope was Christ's vicar on earth and the bishops were the pope's vicars across the world. In turn, the bishops were assisted by priests under them, and the laity was at the bottom. Particularly concerning the bishops, the pre-conciliar teaching was that "some bishops from various countries could be designated by the episcopal conferences and appointed by the

Holy See as members or consultors of the various sacred congregations within the Roman Curia".[19]

During the Second Vatican Council, the understanding of Church developed, emphasizing the community of all the baptized. Bishops and priests are called to ministry, and in particular the bishops form a college, exercising "their own [not a delegated] authority for the good of their own faithful and indeed of the whole Church".[20] On 16 October 1963, Bishop Thomas Holland, speaking on behalf of the English bishops, asked that this doctrine of collegiality be immediately put into practice by the creation of a central organization made up of bishops appointed from around the world. "This was the first time that the Council Hall heard the proposal to establish what we call today the Synod of Bishops ... [and thereafter] the proposal was repeated seventeen times in various forms."[21]

Afterwards, the *motu proprio* (that is to say on the pope's own initiative) *Apostolica solicitudo* formally established the Synod of Bishops. The conciliar document *Christus Dominus* included the words, the Synod "will be representative of the whole Catholic episcopate, will bear testimony to the participation of all the bishops in hierarchical communion in the care of the universal Church".[22] The bishops voted on this text at the 138th general meeting held on 29 September 1965, with 2,171 votes in favour, eight against and three void. Bishop Holland's contribution from the floor was to have far-reaching consequences in the self-understanding of both the Church and the bishops.

In 1986, Geoffrey Chapman published *Vatican II by Those Who Were There*, to which Bishop Holland contributed. In that text, he described Vatican II as the experience of a lifetime—not to be missed at any price and not to be repeated in any of the delegates' lifetimes. Holland described the council as a pastoral experience, human and humanizing and superbly staged and paced. Also, it was, Bishop Holland said, a controlled experience within which the Holy Spirit was to be found.

Although Bishop Holland expected to succeed to the See of Portsmouth, he became involved in what the *Guardian* newspaper called "a game of episcopal musical chairs, which was understood to reflect the influence of the newly appointed Archbishop Heenan of Westminster"[23] (and of course we may observe again that Heenan knew Holland well from

CMS days). Bishop Holland was translated by Pope Paul VI to the See of Salford, succeeding Bishop George Beck (1904–78), on 3 September 1964. Beck had been translated to Liverpool, to replace Heenan who had gone to Westminster, and indeed it was Archbishop Beck who enthroned Bishop Holland in Salford Cathedral just nine days later on 12 September 1964. Luncheon at the racecourse restaurant followed afterwards. Bishop Holland took the Episcopal motto *Adiutor Gaudii Vestri*, a minor paraphrase of the end of the first chapter of the Second Letter to the Corinthians, "*adiutores sumus gaudii vestri*", meaning "we work with you (we are your helpers) for your joy" (RSV), or "we are fellow workers with you for your happiness" (JB).[24]

Bishop Holland took up residence in Wardley Hall, then home of the Bishops of Salford, and the first two years of his ministry were largely occupied by the third and fourth sessions of the Second Vatican Council. No longer an assistant bishop but a diocesan bishop, Holland was now a full Council Father and his accommodation at the *Venerabile* reflected this: no longer a lodger on Cardinal Heard's corridor, but the occupant of a spacious apartment vacated by his predecessor.

In December 1964, Bishop Holland attended the Eucharistic Congress in Bombay, meeting again his former colleague, now Cardinal Gracias, and Pope Paul VI, who also attended, and bequeathed the white Rolls Royce in which he had travelled to Mother Teresa, to help fund her charitable work. Bishop Holland returned from Bombay via the Holy Land.

Holland's 19 years as Bishop of Salford cannot be adequately narrated here, but his principal ambition was to create a diocese united in faith and worship—to emphasize and foster spiritual neighbourliness, especially in the face of the new high-rise tower blocks. Bishop Holland was concerned that jungles were being created rather than communities, and worked with the city planning office and housing authorities. He wrote: "I made a nuisance of myself at the Town Hall."[25]

Having said that, Bishop Holland also worked closely with the civic authorities and writes warmly of the Lord Mayors and the City Councillors. He was also involved with various town-twinning events and recalls making new friends from Le Mans and Paderborn (twinned with Bolton). Cardinal Josyf Slipyj of the Ukrainian Greek Catholic Church also visited, wearing his full regalia.

Bishop Holland's obituary in *The Tablet* speaks particularly of his concern for matters of human life and dignity and of his special concern for education. "He mounted a public protest in the Manchester Free Trade Hall against David Steel's Abortion Bill, engaging other Christians and Jews in his support, and he also spoke out against pornography." He reorganized and amalgamated Catholic schools across the diocese and was said to have been at home with children. "He loved the reunion of the Catholic Handicapped Children's Fellowship and left the royalties on his memoir to the Children's Rescue Society."[26]

Perhaps one of the high points, or one of the most memorable events, was welcoming Pope (now Saint) John Paul II to Manchester during the pontiff's visit to the United Kingdom in the summer of 1982. In the end it was a great success, but was nearly cancelled since the United Kingdom, at that time, was in conflict with Argentina over the Falkland Islands. Following a frantic diplomatic effort, compromise was reached whereby Pope John Paul II visited both the UK and Argentina. The high point of the UK trip was perhaps the service in Canterbury Cathedral jointly presided over by His Holiness and Archbishop Runcie and the subsequent signing of a Common Declaration of Unity.

Two Catholic Lord Mayors of Manchester had personally invited the pope to Manchester in papal audiences, and Manchester was indeed included in the schedule with Mass being celebrated on 31 May 1982 in Heaton Park, the largest municipal park in Europe. Indeed, the Mass was said to be the largest ever gathering in the history of northern England.

The theme of the pope's six-day visit was the seven sacraments, an idea proposed by Michael Bowen, Archbishop of Southwark. One of the most memorable images of the visit was the day when the pope visited St George's Cathedral in Southwark, which had been transformed into a giant hospital ward for the day, to celebrate the sacrament of the sick and a Mass for the sick. The day itself was "a moment of great joy for the archbishop, and was always recalled by the pope whenever the two met in Rome".[27]

Within the theme of the celebration of the sacraments, the pope also celebrated an ordination Mass at Heaton Park in Manchester on 31 May, and 12 deacons were to be selected to be ordained priest by the Holy Father. In his homily, he said to them:

> You must be men of God, his close friends. You must develop daily patterns of prayer, and penance must be a regular part of your life. Prayer and penance will help you appreciate more deeply that the strength of your ministry is found in the Lord and not in human resources.[28]

Additionally, the locals were thrilled when the Holy Father made reference to St Ambrose Barlow OSB (*b*.1585), a Lancashire martyr who gave his life for the faith in 1641 (and whose head, at the time, was kept and venerated in the bishop's house, on the landing).

Bishop Holland reached his seventy-fifth birthday on 11 June 1983 and as is customary, submitted his resignation to the pope. His resignation was accepted by Pope (now Saint) John Paul II on 22 June 1983, but he would retain some oversight of the diocese until April 1984, when his successor, Bishop Patrick Kelly, was installed. Bishop Holland retired to Nazareth House in Prestwich, beginning, so it is said, on the very same day, the writing of his memoirs, which incidentally he dedicated to his beloved auxiliary, Bishop Geoffrey Burke.

Bishop Holland died in Nazareth House, Prestwich, Manchester, on 31 September 1999, aged 91 years. He is buried in Salford Cathedral. His simple tombstone, which bears his coat of arms and motto, reads: "Please Pray for Thomas Holland, VIII Bishop of Salford, RIP."

In his obituary in the *Guardian* newspaper, he was described as a good man, motivated by a sense of duty, never dull and with a sense of humour. Elsewhere it was noted that his impish sense of fun carried him through many awkward moments. Having said that, the *Guardian* also characterized him as "inhibited by a single-minded loyalty to what he conceived to be the will of the pope. The resulting over-cautious timidity meant his diocese was never in the forefront of post-conciliar renewal."[29]

By way of conclusion, I want to suggest that Bishop Holland's long life was characterized by the variety and indeed the sheer quantity of things he did: the scope and the international reach of his ministry. He was clearly very academically able and was involved in seminary teaching for nine years, concluding with a spell as acting rector at the English College in Lisbon. He went on to serve as a military chaplain, being decorated for his bravery. One might be forgiven for thinking that after this he might have returned to a quiet life in academia, but he then embarked on travels to India and beyond. Indeed, travel was to be an integral part of his life, and in addition to visiting much of Europe, he also visited India, the Holy Land, New Zealand, and of course made multiple trips to Rome.

After port chaplaincy work, he then undertook a new challenge working with the Catholic Missionary Society for a further nine years before being appointed as the secretary to the Apostolic Delegate. In a modern world, we might imagine that having passed his fiftieth birthday and led a full life, some consideration of an early retirement might not be inappropriate, but not for Thomas Holland. He was elevated to the purple and served as a bishop for a further 23 years. It is surely a mark of the energy and the dynamism of the man that he also lived for another 16 years after his official retirement.

Notes

1   Kenny, *A Path from Rome*, p. 23.

2   Ibid., p. 31.

3   Thomas Holland, *For Better and for Worse* (Salford: Salford Diocese, 1989), p. 15.

4   Ibid., p. 37.

5   Ibid., p. 45.

6   Ibid., p. 55.

7   Ibid., p. 122.

8   Cf. John Heenan, *Not the Whole Truth* (London: Hodder & Stoughton, 1971), p. 299.

9   Ibid., p. 306.

10 Holland, *For Better and for Worse*, p. 168.

11 Ibid., p. 176.

12 Ibid., p. 195.

13 Ibid., p. 197.

14   Cormac Murphy-O'Connor, *An English Spring* (London: Bloomsbury, 2015), p. 51.

15   Gerard Dwyer, *Diocese of Portsmouth: Past and Present* (Portsmouth: Portsmouth Diocesan Centenary Committee, 1981), p. 115.

16   Ibid.

17   Holland, *For Better and for Worse*, p. 250.

18   Yves Congar, *My Journal of the Council*, tr. Mary John Ronayne OP and Mary Cecily Boulding OP (Collegeville, MN: Liturgical Press, 2012), pp. 378–9.

19   Bonaventure Kloppenburg, *Ecclesiology of Vatican II* (Chicago, IL: Franciscan Herald Press, 1974), pp. 205–6.

20   Ibid., p. 207 and cf. *Lumen gentium* §22–3.

21   Ibid., p. 208.

22   Cf. ibid., p. 211 and cf. *Christus Dominus* §5.

23   *Guardian*, 12 October 1999.

24   2 Corinthians 1:24.

25   Holland, *For Better and for Worse*, p. 239.

26   *The Tablet,* 9 October 1999, p. 1378.

27   Quoted in Bowen's Obituary in *The Tablet*, 31 October 2019.

28   Peter Jennings and Eamonn McCabe, *The Pope in Britain* (London: The Bodley Head, 1982), p. 85.

29   *Guardian*, 12 October 1999.

5

Derek John Harford Worlock (1965–76)

Archbishop King's auxiliary, Bishop Holland, might well have been expected to succeed him but, as we have seen, he was translated to Salford a year before King died, and it was Derek Worlock who was appointed the fifth Bishop of Portsmouth in succession to Archbishop King.

Clifford Longley has described Worlock as a central figure, and arguably *the* central figure, in the story of the post-war English Catholic Church, and in his memoir *An English Spring*, Cardinal Cormac Murphy-O'Connor described Worlock's reputation as a force of nature. He says at the time of his appointment to the See of Portsmouth—unlike all of his predecessors except Bishop Vertue, he had not previously been an auxiliary—a frisson passed through the clergy of the diocese. Worlock had been secretary to three cardinals and attended all four sessions of the Second Vatican Council. It is not altogether surprising, then, that Worlock's time in Portsmouth was relatively brief, and he was in due course translated to be Archbishop of Liverpool, for which he is better known.

In a spirit of cooperation which was somewhat unusual at the time, Bishop Worlock worked very closely with his Anglican counterpart in Liverpool, Bishop David Sheppard, for the common good of the city. On the night that Bishop Worlock arrived in Liverpool, Bishop Sheppard visited him and took him a bottle of wine, and the two quickly established a close working relationship and a close friendship too. They sometimes even preached together, the one concluding the thoughts of the other. In 1988, they co-authored the book *Better Together* and later *With Hope in Our Hearts* (1996), which explained their principle: "Do everything together except the things that conscience forces us to do apart." Their remarkable collaboration is commemorated in a bronze sculpture by

Stephen Broadbent, which is located in Hope Street, the road that runs between the two cathedrals. The sculpture is officially known as the Sheppard–Worlock Statue, but affectionately known by "scousers" as "fish and chips", as the two went together so well and were always in the newspapers!

Derek John Harford Warlock was born on 4 February 1920 at 7F Grove End Road in St John's Wood in London, in a flat overlooking Lord's Cricket Ground. His father was Harford Worlock, a journalist who later became a political agent for the Conservative Party; and his mother was Dora née Hoblyn, also something of a political activist and one-time suffragette. Indeed, it was something of their shared socio-political outlook, not to mention common interests in music and the arts, which brought them together.

Derek had an elder brother, Peter (*b.*1915), who was killed during the Second World War, and a twin sister, Patricia. His parents were initially Anglican, and Harford Worlock at one time considered becoming an Anglican clergyman, but both parents converted to Catholicism in July 1913, while they were "dating". A year later, they were married, and young Derek was raised as a Catholic. He and his twin sister were underweight at birth, and so the following week, on 12 February, Father Clement Parsons was called in to baptize the two babies. Legend has it that a rose bowl was used as an impromptu font; counter-legend suggested a pudding basin, which Worlock always vigorously denied. Either way, Worlock later claimed it was the most important day of his life and professed that he wished to be a priest from the very earliest age.

Dora, Worlock's mother described the twins in her journal:

> They were really fascinating babies, and I was not the only one to admire them. Patricia had absolutely golden hair, lots of it, with a donkey fringe. Derek's hair was thick, a sort of reddy-brown when he was born, and curly ... Derek's eyes were grey like mine and Peter's and he had a rounder face and not such a straight nose.[1]

Derek attended a local kindergarten in London and later Priory House Preparatory School in Swiss Cottage. A school report from 1926 rates him as "very good" or "excellent" in nearly all subjects. In 1927, he and his sister made their first communion and later that same year were confirmed at Pentecost at the hands of Bishop Joseph Butt (1869–1944, auxiliary in Westminster). It is said the reception of these sacraments strengthened young Derek's resolve to be a priest.

When he was aged nine, the family moved to Winchester, where Derek attended Winton House Preparatory School (founded 1863), just outside the city centre. The educational standard was high, and Derek learnt the rudiments of Latin and Greek. Spelling and grammar were drummed into him, and he engaged in a wide variety of sporting activities, particularly rugby at which he excelled, although in one rugby accident he broke his arm. The only drawback of this traditional Anglican school was that Derek was a Catholic, and very probably the only Catholic—and one who wanted to be a priest!

After Winton House Worlock went to St Edmund's College, Ware, which was, at the time, a school-cum-seminary for the Archdiocese of Westminster. Worlock received the encouragement and indeed the recommendation of Bishop Butt, who had confirmed him and was something of a family friend. Despite Bishop Cotter's disapproval, with Butt's support, Worlock went to St Edmund's in the Lent term 1934 as a Westminster student.

At St Edmund's, Worlock continued to progress academically. He was described as muscular and robust and also continued to play rugby with great determination, becoming captain of his house team and senior prefect in his house too. He was an all-rounder, intelligent and hardworking, winning prizes in Greek and Latin. He was considered to have integrity and a dry wit by his contemporaries, some of whom also remember him as reserved if not aloof, but he was not without friends. His closest friend was Bernard Fisher (the "Fish"), who was later ordained a priest alongside Worlock, and the two remained brother priests and close friends throughout their lives.

Worlock also quickly took St Edmund, the patron of the college, as his own. "Having prayed to Mary in the Lady Chapel, I would go each morning and evening to the shrine and would recite the prayer 'O glorious Saint Edmund, most highly exalted among the friends of

God' which I rapidly came to know by heart and which I still recite each morning."[2]

Parenthetically, we may note that St Edmund, variously known as St Edmund of Abingdon (after where he was born in Oxfordshire) and St Edmund of Canterbury (after where he was archbishop), was a thirteenth-century Oxford scholar-turned-cleric, who became Treasurer at Salisbury Cathedral and later Archbishop of Canterbury, where he had a difficult relationship with King Henry III. He died on his way to Rome and is buried at Pontigny Abbey in north Burgundy. He is to be distinguished from St Edmund King and Martyr, of Bury St Edmund's fame, and is also the secondary patron of the Diocese of Portsmouth, along with Our Lady of the Immaculate Conception.

Worlock went up to the senior seminary, and when he was 19, the war broke out, but, as was licit, Derek elected to continue his clerical training rather than serve in the armed forces. In the autumn term of 1940, Derek received the tonsure, which at that time marked entry into the clerical state. As part of the "war effort", he was given the task of College Air Raid Warden, something of a dangerous job as several bombs fell in the college grounds. The job meant he had to walk around the entire college each evening. "Often I went privately into the college chapel and shrine ... there I would pray to be a priest and also for those who had been in the school with me who had been killed or were missing in action."[3]

Towards the end of his studies, Worlock was ordained to the diaconate at St Edmund's College in June 1943, after a retreat with the Cistercian community at Mount St Bernard near Leicester. Some months later, Worlock became ill with severe sinusitis: a chronic condition which required surgery (a hole was to be drilled in the bone of his nose to clear congestion). He was told he would only ever be fit for gentle and perhaps part-time duties, and that plans to study in Cambridge, and perhaps teach in a seminary, would have to be shelved. Furthermore, and a devastating blow after 11 years of study, Worlock was also told by his college president that he would have to go to hospital and would have to forget about being ordained alongside his fellow students—for the time being at least. On the night before his departure for hospital, he secretly went to the shrine chapel, kissed the relic of St Edmund and placed it against his head, praying for ordination. Meanwhile, his fellow students started a novena of prayer for his recovery, and a blue nun (a sister of the Little Company of Mary) named Sister Raphael, who was nursing him, fortified him with a daily glass of Guinness.

Whether it was the novena or the Guinness, Worlock's surgery was successful, and he was discharged from hospital the day before the ordination retreat began and was ordained priest in Westminster Cathedral, alongside his fellow deacons, for the Archdiocese of Westminster by Archbishop (and later Cardinal) Bernard Griffin on 3 June 1944 (three days before D-Day). Father Worlock celebrated his first Mass the next day in his home parish of St Peter's in Winchester with Mgr Mullarkey as his assistant priest, and then he visited his family in Itchen Abbas. The war years prevented Worlock from studying in Rome, and in later life it is said he regretted not having been able to study at Cambridge.

After ordination, he was sent to be curate at the Church of Our Lady of Victories in Kensington under Canon James Walton. The church has historic links going back for centuries and was re-established after the Reformation (as the Kensington Mission) in 1794. From 1869 until the building of Westminster Cathedral (in 1903), it was the pro-cathedral for the archdiocese. On 13 September 1940, German bombers struck and four incendiary bombs landed on the roof of the church; within a matter of hours the church was completely devastated and had burned to the ground. Rebuilding was not permitted until after the end of the war, and so OLV found itself as a parish without a church.

However, daily Mass, the focus of Catholic life, and other services continued at first in the Odeon Cinema and then in the Cavendish Furnishings building, which became known informally as St Cavendish's, and elsewhere too. The parish motto at the time was "Survival", and the indefatigable parish priest, Canon James Walton, kept the parish alive. In due course, funds were raised and a striking new church was built to a design by Adrian Gilbert Scott. The new church was opened by Cardinal Godfrey on 16 April 1959 and, most fittingly, later consecrated by the former curate, by now Archbishop of Liverpool, on 26 May 1971, in the presence of Cardinal Heenan. During his curacy, Fr Worlock continued to play rugby on a Saturday afternoon, although his parish priest insisted that he was back in time to hear confessions at 6.30 p.m. When he became the cardinal's secretary, rugby was forbidden him, lest he incapacitate himself with sporting injury.

After his brief curacy, and certainly sooner that he would have liked, Worlock was called to Archbishop's House to be secretary to Cardinal Bernard Griffin (1899–1956). He must have done a good job, since he remained there for the next 20 years, also acting as secretary to Cardinal William Godfrey (1889–1963), and for a short time to Cardinal John Heenan. In 1949, Cardinal Griffin's health deteriorated markedly, when he suffered a stroke leaving him partially paralysed and unable to speak clearly. Fr Worlock wrote many of Griffin's sermons, answered his letters, developed contacts with various Whitehall offices, acted as the Church's *de facto* press officer, and could very much be seen to be the power behind the throne. It was most probably Worlock's intention to protect Cardinal Godfrey, and he probably believed the Westminster clergy were unaware of the part that he played. But, in fact, they were well aware and some resented Worlock's role, and this would have future repercussions. It is worth noting that resignation was not an option for Cardinal Griffin at the time, so it was also Worlock who masterminded the celebrations for the centenary of the restoration of the Catholic hierarchy in 1950.

The Hierarchy Centenary Congress culminated in a week of high-profile events at the end of September. Seven cardinals as well as numerous bishops and archbishops were involved and the ailing Cardinal Griffin presided and was commissioned to act on behalf of Pope Pius XII "in Our name and at all public gatherings and sacred ceremonies, and enhance the splendour of them with the dignity of the Roman purple".[4] Remarkably, at the High Mass in Wembley Stadium a message from the pope expressed his sentiments of profound esteem for King George VI and Queen Elizabeth. Some commentators have suggested that the 1950s saw the apogee of the integration of Catholic life into the civic life of the nation.

Described as tall, slim, bespectacled and dignified, Worlock was considered aloof by some, but was efficient and perceptive. He was created Privy Chamberlain (in other words monsignor, although this class of monsignor was abolished by Pope Paul VI in 1968) and afterwards Domestic Prelate in 1953. In 1951 Cardinal Griffin had a coronary thrombosis, and in June 1956, while he was preaching to

Catholic holders of the Victoria Cross, he had another heart attack. He went, with Mgr Worlock, to Polzeath in Cornwall to convalesce and in the hope that he would recover; but he died on 20 August 1956, having been fortified by the last rites of the Church administered by Worlock, his ever-present assistant.

Griffin was succeeded by Archbishop (and later Cardinal) William Godfrey, whose secretary Worlock also became. Significantly, Worlock accompanied Godfrey to Rome on multiple occasions. There was the funeral of Pope Pius XII and then the coronation of Pope John XXIII in November 1958. Worlock also accompanied Archbishop Godfrey, who was a member of one of the Council's preparatory commissions, and he also attended all four sessions of the Second Vatican Council; an experience that would surely prepare him for future high office. Significantly too, Worlock kept a diary at the council meetings, dictated last thing at night to a tape recorder. These recordings would later become the basis for Clifford Longley's book *The Worlock Archive* and are a valuable historical resource more generally.

An amusing story is connected with the convening of the Second Vatican Council by Pope Saint John XXIII. Worlock recalled having been in Rome for the coronation of Pope John XXIII, and after Christmas in the UK, he visited Archbishop Godfrey at Archbishop's House, one evening in January 1959:

> As I pulled up, Bishop Cashman [auxiliary in Westminster at the time and later Bishop of Arundel and Brighton] came down the front steps and laughing said, "You had better hurry up and pack your bag: you are off to Rome again." This remark took me completely by surprise and my first reaction was that the Pope must be dead. The bishop however added: "John XXIII has really done it this time. He's called an Ecumenical Council."[5]

At this stage it was, in fact, just an announcement of the pope's intention to call a council and the formal summons was not made until *Humanae salutis* was promulgated on 25 December 1961.

Worlock was also appointed a *peritus* (or theological advisor) to Bishop John Petit (1895–1973) of Menevia, working for the Commission for the Lay Apostolate, and he also became involved in the drafting and redrafting of the Pastoral Constitution on the Church in the Modern World, *Gaudium et spes*. Finally, Worlock also formed a friendship with Bishop Karol Wojtyla from Krakow, later Pope John Paul II; they were the same age, both having been born in 1920, although Worlock was some 16 weeks older.

Godfrey's time as archbishop was a time of great Catholic expansion but Godfrey himself was considered remote and made little impact. He wrote a couple of books and is remembered for his "poodle" pastoral letter, where he suggested that pets should join their owners on days of fasting. He wrote: "A plump and pampered poodle might run all the more gaily after a reduced diet on simpler fare." This observation unfortunately coincided with Cruft's Dog Show that year and infuriated many dog lovers around the country. Again, Worlock did much to support Cardinal Godfrey, but clerical wits of the time "were said to amuse themselves with such questions as 'why is this man Godfrey signing Monsignor Worlock's letters?'"[6]

A final little anecdote is that under Cardinal Griffin, an evening celebration of the Mass had been permitted in Westminster Cathedral, even if Griffin had consented to this reluctantly. Cardinal Godfrey, when he arrived, instructed Worlock to put an end to the practice. However, "realizing that this would incur a good deal of wrath from regular Mass-goers, he managed to stall and the services went on as before".[7] From this, it would appear that the diplomatic skills for which Worlock would become well known were probably learnt, and were indeed already in operation, when Worlock was secretary to Cardinals Griffin and Godfrey in Westminster.

After just over six years at Westminster, Cardinal Godfrey died and he was succeeded by Archbishop (and later Cardinal) Heenan. It was time for Worlock to move on. He later reported that the new archbishop scarcely used him and never told him what he was up to. He later came to recognize that Heenan perhaps realized that there was only room for one leader in Archbishop's House. Furthermore, it is said that on a personal level, Worlock did not like Heenan, a sentiment that was fully reciprocated.

A rumour circulated that Worlock might be appointed coadjutor bishop of Menevia, but he was sent to be parish priest of the Church of St Mary and St Michael on Commercial Road in Stepney and was appointed dean of the area. This was a tough parish in a run-down part of east London, and many of Worlock's friends and colleagues could not understand the appointment, thinking that after years of faithful service as the cardinals' secretary he deserved something better.

But it seems that Worlock himself exercised some degree of choice in the matter and was keen to gain some real pastoral experience. Years later he observed that something of a conversion was "due to those months at Stepney, to the priests that I was with then, and the laity, especially the dockers and their families, with whom I worked in undoubtedly the happiest time of my life, March 1964 to October 1965".[8]

So not only was he happy, but he underwent something of a "conversion", not in a mystical sense, but he came to see in a real and grounded way what the implementation of the Second Vatican Council might look like. In Stepney, Worlock had the opportunity to discover what the theological reflections that he had been so closely involved in, in Rome, might actually mean in an everyday Catholic parish. Worlock's work with the Commission for the Lay Apostolate would have direct consequences too.

In Stepney, Worlock began to get involved with the lay leaders of the Young Christian Workers (YCW) movement, contributing to spiritual formation and catechesis. He had first come across YCW at seminary when he was lectured in sociology by Fr Bernard Good, who was himself closely involved in the YCW. Worlock became the chaplain of the local YCW, attending a monthly meeting, celebrating the Mass for them and providing continuing spiritual counsel. In the parish, he established new team programmes and "team living" based around pastoral visiting and the creation of small groups. The groups grew and the sense of community within the parish swelled. In 18 months, the Mass attendance rose from under 1,000 to 2,800, in a parish with a population of 7,000.

Not only was the parish transformed, but for our story, Worlock was transformed too. He wrote that a move from the marble halls of Archbishop's House put the spotlight on things for others, and he became (politically) increasingly left-leaning, to the consternation of some of his friends. With the privilege of hindsight, one can see how Worlock's involvement with cardinals and his experiences in Rome *combined* with his work in Stepney formed a man who was ready for the next stage in his life. Worlock told a Catholic news reporter: "Whatever the future, nothing can eradicate the inspiration of my time in Stepney." Additionally, we may note that Worlock has also been categorized as a priest rather more focused on, motivated by and enthusiastic about, the social teachings of the Church as opposed to more theoretical doctrinal issues.

After just 18 months in Stepney, Worlock was appointed Bishop of Portsmouth (on 18 October 1965) by Pope Paul VI. It is said that the initial plan was still to send Worlock to Menevia and Father Langton Fox, rector of the seminary at Wonersh, was to be appointed Bishop of Portsmouth. In the event, and for reasons which are still not completely clear, they were swapped round, and Langton Fox went to Menevia (first as the auxiliary and then as the ordinary) and Worlock was appointed to Portsmouth. Cardinal Heenan almost certainly had something to do with this and is alleged to have said to Worlock in private: "After the next session of the Council you will not be returning to Stepney. You are likely to be a bishop, but you need not imagine that you are going to be one of my auxiliaries here. You will be much further away."[9]

Worlock was ordained bishop in the cathedral in Portsmouth on 21 December 1965, the feast of St Thomas the Apostle, by Cardinal Heenan assisted by Bishop Edward Ellis (Nottingham) and Bishop William Power (Atigonish in Nova Scotia). Bishop Holland was also present and assisted too. Archbishop Cyril Cowderoy (Southwark) preached the homily. Some 2,000 people attended the ceremonies, including 16 bishops and archbishops and 280 priests; the Anglican Bishops of Portsmouth and of Winchester, the Lord Mayor of Portsmouth and the Mayor of Winchester, and Mr Maurice Foley MP also attended. On the evening of the installation, there was a reception for the new bishop in the Guildhall attended by the Lord Mayor of the city and other dignitaries and many of Worlock's friends and family, including a loyal contingent from Stepney. The *Portsmouth Evening News* carried a full-page photograph of the new bishop in his cathedral, taken by staff photographer, Trevor Upton.[10]

Worlock took the episcopal motto *Caritas Christi Eluceat*, meaning "let (or may) Christ's love shine out". This is a quotation from the Council's

Decree on the Pastoral Office of Bishops, and Worlock explained that it was his own personal mission statement; it was in his mind what the role of a bishop should be. He wanted to form members of the Church to look *outwards*: to concern themselves with the world rather than looking inwards at themselves.

Bishop Worlock set up home in the now renovated Bishop's House in Portsmouth, although initially there was no central heating and the house was unfurnished. Three Sisters of Mercy ran the household, and within six months Worlock had appointed Fr Cormac Murphy-O'Connor as his secretary. It is said that the nun deputed to cook was something of a novice in the kitchen and one day produced sausage rolls served with baked beans. Not wanting to discourage her, the clerics thanked her and said how much they had enjoyed the meal. Sometime later, Bishop Worlock invited guests for dinner including the Mayor and an Admiral of the Fleet. The finest crockery and cutlery had been laid out and Murphy-O'Connor had selected some suitably fine wine. After the *hors d'oeuvre*, sister proudly produced her signature dish: sausage rolls and baked beans! Derek's face was a study, but the Admiral rose to the occasion. "Wonderful! What a splendid change. Though I have to say, he said, looking over at me [Murphy-O'Connor] 'I'm not convinced this wine is an entirely suitable complement to these magnificent baked beans.'"[11]

Worlock's principal task was to implement the reforms, or communicate the insights, of the Second Vatican Council and when he was asked what aspects of the council he intended to implement he replied, "the lot". Within a short time, every parish had a lay council, every deanery had a Deanery Pastoral Council, and these all fed into the Diocesan Pastoral Council. Bishop Worlock established eight diocesan commissions, concerning themselves with education, sites and buildings, ecumenism, liturgy, youth, social service and the pastoral council secretariat. The 1976 *Diocesan Yearbook* stated:

> The Portsmouth Diocesan Council is made up of priest, religious and lay representatives from each deanery in the diocese and of representatives from Catholic organizations. Each year groups in all the parishes study some matter of concern to the whole diocese

> and then meet with the bishop in Plenary Assembly to try to work
> out what is to be diocesan policy in that matter.[12]

The subject of concern in 1976, for example, was "Adult Education", and the Plenary Assembly met at LSU College of Education in Southampton on 3 April 1976.

In accordance with the Council's recommendations, in 1967, Park Place Pastoral Centre was opened to facilitate training: spiritual, doctrinal and practical for Catholics in southern England and for the Diocese of Portsmouth in particular. Worlock wrote: "The follower of Christ, no matter how enthusiastic, needs training how to present his wares."[13] By 1974, the diocese was structured anew and was considered to be the shop window of the Second Vatican Council. Additionally, during the course of his Portsmouth episcopate some 30 new churches were built, and almost every church in the diocese was reordered to bring them all into line with the new liturgical norms.

Worlock quickly established something of a routine. On most Sundays, he conducted parish visitations, preaching and perhaps confirming. These visits were often extended into Mondays, when he liked to visit schools and the children of the parish. He was greatly occupied with preparing speeches and sermons, preparing for meetings and writing letters—including regular letters to the clergy of the diocese. Worlock also got to know the Labour MP for Portsmouth at the time, Frank Judd. They often made joint visits to homes and places of work combining religion and politics; and Judd's left-leaning policies fitted well with the social teaching of the Church. Worlock claimed that he learnt a lot from Judd, particularly his ability to converse with and question people with whom he was talking.

Bishop Worlock grew in stature by his calm handling of the turmoil over the papal encyclical *Humanae vitae*, published in July 1968. The full story is a rather long and convoluted one, but in brief, Bishop Worlock reassured doubting clergy and handled a hostile press with calm statesmanlike words. He produced a pastoral letter, as did many of the other bishops, and struck a balance by "taking into account Catholic moral teaching regarding situations that are objectively sinful, but also the subjective dispositions of faithful Christian men and women".[14]

Later Worlock suggested that *Humanae vitae* was "not the acid test of Christianity", which helped to put the teaching into a wider context. At one time, when Worlock was away, one Portsmouth priest was suspended by the vicar general for speaking out against the encyclical, but when Worlock returned, he was quietly reinstated.

Ecumenism would be the defining hallmark of Worlock's time in Liverpool, but his commitment to it began long before. In Portsmouth, Worlock set about building ecumenical cooperation and friendship. Meetings were set up where clergy of all the different denominations in a particular area might meet together. This is commonplace now, but at the time it was revolutionary. In a Mass for Christian unity at Holy Rood Church, he suggested that the Council's Decree on Christian Unity gave a clear charter for immediate action, and in a sermon, he spelt this out:

> Let us be clear that by our joint activity we mean such matters as housing, care of old people, care of the poor and inadequate families, world hunger and international peace ... We must work together for the community at large not just our own Catholic community ... Guided by charity and the search for truth we need have no fear as we move steadily forward on our path to unity.[15]

Worlock was apparently quite a one for meetings, which he chaired with efficiency and authority; he was a master of the minutes and the agenda and always followed due procedure. He was a good organizer and a natural leader. Indeed, Cardinal Basil Hume was supposed to have said that Worlock was the only man he knew who genuinely read all the small print; such was his attention to detail. It is also said that he slept little, even that he was an insomniac, and he was always up early in the morning. He was hardworking and wanted to be involved in everything. During his time as Bishop of Portsmouth, 11 new churches were opened. Worlock was austere and ate and drank little but was a great fixer and broker of deals and compromises in difficult situations. He travelled a lot for meetings and parish visitations. Cormac Murphy-O'Connor remarked that after serving Worlock for four years as his secretary he was exhausted from all the travelling.

I mentioned above that one of the significant developments of the council, and initiated by a contribution from Bishop Holland, was that bishops were to be seen as having a collective responsibility for the Church across the world. In the document *Christus Dominus*, bishops were encouraged to promote works of evangelization and the apostolate, encouraging where possible some of their own priests to go to serve on missions overseas. Now Bishop Worlock had his own diocese in order, this was a matter that he could turn to.

In 1974, Bishop Worlock established a link with Bishop Paul Verdzekov, and the Dioceses of Portsmouth and Bamenda, in the United Republic of Cameroon in West Africa, were twinned as a practical demonstration of the teachings of the Council. Bishop Worlock consulted with his own diocese, with the Diocese of Bamenda and with the Mill Hill Missionaries who had worked in the region, and in the autumn of 1975 three Portsmouth priests set out for the diocese of Bamenda. Others followed over the years. Worlock's intention was that there would be six priests in Bamenda at any one time, each serving a six-year overlapping term. Worlock himself also made several visits to Cameroon, the first in 1975, and these left an indelible impression on him.

The Second Vatican Council reinstated the permanent diaconate in principle, and Pope Paul VI restored it in practice by the publication (in 1967) of his apostolic letter *Sacrum diaconatus ordinem*. Bishop Worlock embraced the new provision, and in 1974 he ordained Patrick Taylor, a married man and a business executive, as the first permanent deacon in the Diocese of Portsmouth. Deacon Taylor was given pastoral responsibility in the group ministry in Basingstoke, and he would go on to write *Called to Serve*, a little book about the permanent diaconate published in 2007.

Cardinal Heenan, Archbishop of Westminster, died on 7 November 1975, and Worlock, surely on account of his experience, efficiency and hard work was considered to be something of a front-runner in Rome, although there was said to be some opposition amongst the Westminster clergy themselves. In the event, Abbot Basil Hume of Ampleforth was appointed to Westminster, and a week before this was announced, in February 1976, Worlock was appointed to be Archbishop of Liverpool. What was surely highly unusual is that the Anglican Bishop of Liverpool,

David Sheppard had been invited to dinner by the papal nuncio, Bruno Heim, and quizzed for an hour or so, about the pastoral needs and priorities of Liverpool. It has been remarked that Worlock was probably the first, and perhaps the only, Catholic bishop to be appointed on the advice of an Anglican one!

Clifford Longley summarized Worlock's time in Portsmouth as follows:

> The verdict on his Portsmouth decade must be that he achieved most of what he wanted but learned less than he might have done. Unlike what was to happen in Liverpool there was no particular ecumenical partnership forged in that period, partly because Portsmouth Roman Catholic diocese covered all or part of about six Anglican dioceses. . . . The Portsmouth years did not see any great development on his thinking on issues of politics and social justice domestically—it took the influence of David Sheppard to trigger that—though he was keen to see the success of CAFOD . . . Worlock had not really got to grips with the deep conservatism of old-guard Catholic clergy educated before the Second Vatican Council and not very interested in finding out about it or seeing what it had to do with them.[16]

Worlock was installed in his new cathedral on 19 March 1976. Pope Paul VI gave him a double mandate: to work for the poor and unemployed in the city and to prevent Liverpool from becoming "another Belfast". There was political instability and division in the city and the "Irish Troubles" were never far away. It is said that Worlock was disappointed, on a personal level, not to have been appointed to Westminster, but publicly he insisted he was very pleased with Basil Hume's appointment and his own translation to Liverpool, where he could have a real pastoral role rather than a predominantly national one. With characteristic gusto Worlock threw himself into his new role in Liverpool.

As this book is about the Catholic bishops of Portsmouth, I am not going to consider Worlock's remarkable time in Liverpool in detail. I have already referred to his unprecedented ecumenical relationship with

Bishop David Sheppard, but there are two other particular events, which have been described as pinnacles of his episcopate, I want to mention.

The first was the huge National Pastoral Congress held in Liverpool in 1980, which was organized and meticulously planned by Archbishop Worlock. There was a very extensive pre-congress consultation, and the results of parish meetings fed into deanery and diocesan forums, which in turn formed the agenda for the congress, although the broad theme was to discuss what the Second Vatican Council meant for ordinary English Catholics in the pew.

Over the long Bank Holiday weekend in May 1980, 2,115 Catholics convened from all over the country, including 42 bishops, 255 clergy and 150 religious. Worlock was asked whether he was not nervous about inviting so many people, especially the laity, to gather and express their views openly and honestly. His reply was: "Don't you believe in the Holy Spirit in the Church?"[17] The congress met in seven sectors, each devoted to one of the themes that had emerged from the grassroots consultations. These were: co-responsibility and relationships, ordained ministries, family and society, evangelization, Christian education and formation, witness, and justice.

Each sector submitted a report of their discussions, and these were combined to form an overall summary of the meeting which ran to 50 pages and was titled: *Liverpool 1980: Official Report of the National Pastoral Congress*. A few months after the congress, another document, *The Easter People*, appeared, billed as reflections in the light of the congress. This was prepared by Archbishop Worlock himself, with a team of helpers, and the approval of the whole bishops' conference. Basil Hume said: "It expressed our growing awareness that we are a single people of God whose pastors and laity have their distinct but complementary ministries within the unique mission of the Church."[18]

It is difficult to assess how fruitful this congress was, and some complained of the lack of follow-up, but in Liverpool certainly, the idea of collaborative ministry, with clergy and laity working side by side, was firmly planted. The appointment of Pat Jones, as the first woman assistant secretary to the English and Welsh Bishops' Conference, was also seen to be a significant consequence of the congress. Finally, 15 years after the congress, in 1995, a working party from the Catholic Bishops'

Conference of England and Wales produced *The Sign We Give*, a report on collaborative ministry, which has been described as inspirational and essential reading for all committed to collaborative ministry; it emphasizes that everyone in the Church is a co-worker under one Lord.[19]

The second event was the papal visit of Pope John Paul II to the United Kingdom in May 1982. In the event, the visit was a great success, but it was nearly cancelled, because in April 1982 Argentina invaded the Falkland Islands in the south Atlantic, and Prime Minister Margaret Thatcher sent a huge naval contingent to claim them back. It was considered inappropriate, to say the least, for the pope to visit a country at war—even an undeclared war—especially when the perceived aggressor, Argentina, was formally a Catholic country. A huge diplomatic effort followed to try and rescue the papal visit to Britain, and in the end this succeeded by arranging papal visits to both Britain and Argentina.

A number of British prelates were involved in the negotiations, not least Cardinal Basil Hume, but not unsurprisingly perhaps Worlock was heavily involved too. It is said that Cardinals Gray and Hume had tried very hard in Rome to defuse the difficult political situation but, it seemed, without success. Archbishop (later Cardinal) Thomas Winning of Glasgow was considering a final attempt to sort things out when he received a telephone call from Archbishop Worlock in Liverpool, and Winning reported that Worlock said: "Tom, let's both of us go to Rome and see if we can sort it out! I've cleared it with my cardinal. Why don't you do the same?"[20]

To cut a bit of a long story short, the two archbishops met at Heathrow, but an air traffic controllers' dispute in Italy looked like scuppering their plans. While they waited, they received a mysterious telephone call saying an Italian Air Force plane was shortly due at Heathrow to collect a senior Italian officer, and seats would be made available for the two archbishops. In the event, the aircraft arrived, but there was no sign of the supposed Italian army general, and as Winning said "we were the only two passengers on board. It was almost like a spy thriller."[21]

Early on the Saturday evening, they arrived at a military airport south of Rome and were whizzed through the traffic into Rome and to the Vatican, where rounds of meetings took place with all the parties involved throughout the evening and into the night. The following morning there

was "the crunch meeting", with Worlock and the others in Pope John
Paul II's private office. Winning relates that he surprisingly received a
telegram from the Inter-Church Committee of the Church of Scotland
which read: "WE REGARD POPE JOHN PAUL II AS PROPHETIC.
IF HE DOES NOT COME WE WILL NO LONGER REGARD HIM
AS PROPHETIC".

The message was passed to the pope who smiled and said that the time
had come to lift the matter above politics, and announced his intention
to visit both countries. "Derek Worlock and Tom Winning retraced their
steps along the corridors. Halfway along, the Archbishop of Liverpool
looked at the Archbishop of Glasgow, winked and laughed delightedly."[22]
Worlock was undoubtedly someone who could make things happen at
the very highest level. Longley elaborated:

> He was the manipulator and fixer, the spin-doctor, the man with
> contacts, the backstairs negotiator and late-night phone-caller,
> the precise minute-taker, the ingenious resolution drafter, the
> committee chairman who could quote standing orders backwards
> (because he wrote them). As they say in politics, he knew where
> the bodies were buried.[23]

Here is not the place to recount the details of the pope's visit to the United
Kingdom, but it should be noted that the pontiff went to Worlock's
cathedral in Liverpool, and to the Anglican Cathedral in Liverpool too.
Pope St John Paul II was applauded all the way up the aisle, and Cardinal
Basil Hume would later remark that "the applause which greeted the
Holy Father remains with me as the most earnest and insistent prayer
for Christian unity that I have ever heard". It almost persuaded Pope
John Paul II that ecumenism in Britain was a popular cause but, more
significantly perhaps, it was a tribute to the cooperation of the two
Liverpool bishops: Worlock and Sheppard.

Archbishop Worlock celebrated the golden jubilee of his priestly
ordination in June 1994. Also in 1994, he received the Freedom of the
City of Liverpool with Bishop David Sheppard. And he was appointed
a Companion of Honour (the highest civil award then accorded to a
Catholic bishop) in the 1996 New Year's Honours List but died eight days

before the planned investiture at Buckingham Palace. Bishop Worlock also received honorary degrees from the Universities of Liverpool, Liverpool John Moore's, Cambridge and Southampton.

In July 1992, Worlock underwent surgery for lung cancer, but complications followed and in the end it got the better of him. His surgeon observed that he bore his disease with a supernatural outlook and great fortitude. He died in Lourdes Hospital, Liverpool, on 8 February 1996, four days after his 76th birthday and one day after the 20th anniversary of his appointment as Archbishop of Liverpool. His funeral was celebrated by Cardinal Basil Hume. Afterwards, The Most Reverend Derek Worlock was buried in the Metropolitan Cathedral of Christ the King in Liverpool, in the St Joseph's Chapel. His tombstone bears the simple inscription:

Derek Worlock CH

1920—1996

Archbishop of Liverpool

1976—1996

One year after his death, Worlock's literary executors, Canon Nicholas France of Portsmouth Diocese and Bishop Vincent Nichols (Westminster), gave the Catholic journalist Clifford Longley unfettered access to all of Worlock's papers and diaries ("a man's life reduced to cardboard boxes"[24]), which resulted in the book *The Worlock Archive* published in 2000. Much of this work concerns itself with the diaries and notes that Worlock kept during the Second Vatican Council, and contains far more detail than can be conveyed here, but a point that particularly emerges and has not yet been mentioned is Worlock's sense of humour.

For all his efficiency and management capabilities, he was a man with a sense of humour too. When he was secretary to the cardinals, he drew amusing cartoons, some of which appeared on homemade Christmas cards which he sent to other bishops' secretaries. He enjoyed anecdotes, and his diaries are sprinkled with them. He wrote humorous sketches and a three-act playlet for the Catholic Scout Guild, and he also penned and sang drily satirical songs, sometimes performed on the traditional last night social of the annual meeting of the National Conference of Priests. One was in memory of his beloved Cardinal Griffin (*b*.1899):

Vintage Year

In 1899 my boy, in 1899
The grapes were very fine, my boy,
a credit to the vine.
But what made it a vintage year
was not the sparkling wine—
A cardinal was born, my boy, in 1899.

(Chorus *ad libitum*: Drink to him, drink to him.)

On 8 February 2011, Worlock's successor in Liverpool, Archbishop Patrick Kelly, celebrated a Mass in memory of Archbishop Worlock, regarded by some as an "honorary scouser", on the fifteenth anniversary of his death. On the Independent Catholic News website, Archbishop Worlock's implementation of the Second Vatican Council in Portsmouth and in Liverpool was emphasized. He renewed parish life, built new churches and made ecumenical relationships his special concern. However, he was not parochial and was a frequent visitor to Rome; his ministry was international and furthermore extended beyond the confines of the Catholic Church. The then Archbishop of Canterbury, George Carey, said that he "touched with grace all the Christian churches of our land", and even Prime Minister John Major observed that "he was a good man in every way—and that is something rare".[25]

Notes

[1]   Quoted in John Furnival and Ann Knowles, *Archbishop Derek Worlock: His Personal Journey* (London: Geoffrey Chapman, 1998), p. 20.

2   From Worlock's diaries, quoted in Longley Clifford, *The Worlock Archive* (London: Geoffrey Chapman, 2000), p. 205.

3   Ibid., p. 206.

4   *Hierarchy Centenary Congress*, p. 8, quoted in Dominic Aidan Bellinger and Stella Fletcher, *Princes of the Church* (Stroud: Sutton Publishing, 2001), p. 157.

5   Longley, *The Worlock Archive*, p. 39–40.

6   Ibid., p. 158.

7   Michael J. Walsh, *The Westminster Cardinals* (London: Burns & Oates), p. 163.

8   Ibid., p. 191.

9   Ibid., p. 207.

10   *Portsmouth Evening News*, 21 December 1965.

11   Cormac Murphy-O'Connor, *An English Spring* (London: Bloomsbury, 2015), p. 66.

12   1976 *Diocesan Year Book*, p. 18.

13   Quoted in Gerard Dwyer, *Diocese of Portsmouth: Past and Present* (Portsmouth: Portsmouth Diocesan Centenary Committee, 1981), p. 122.

14   Murphy-O'Connor, *An English Spring*, p. 78.

15   Quoted in Furnival and Knowles, *Archbishop Derek Worlock: His Personal Journey*, p. 141.

16   Longley, *The Worlock Archive*, p. 274.

17   Kevin T. Kelly, *50 Years Receiving Vatican II* (Dublin: The Columba Press, 2012), p. 79.

18   Derek Worlock's obituary in the *Independent*, 9 February 1996.

19   Cf. Kelly, *50 Years of Receiving Vatican II*, p. 81.

20   Fraser Elder, Martin Gilfeather and George Wilkie, *Always Winning* (Edinburgh: Mainstream Publishing Company, 2001), p. 38.

21   Ibid., p. 40.

22   Ibid., p. 43.

23   Longley, *The Worlock Archive*, p. 2.

24   Ibid., p. 1.

25   Furnival and Knowles, *Archbishop Derek Worlock: His Personal Journey*, p. xiii.

6

Anthony Joseph Emery (1976–88)

Anthony Emery came from a family which has given many priests to the Church: Canon Augustine Emery and Mgr Leonard Emery were his uncles; Bishop Humphrey Bright was his father's cousin, and Provost Henry Yeo was his mother's uncle. Mgr Percival Rees was also related to the family. Father Laurence Emery, who taught at Oscott for a time, was not directly related to the family.[1] It is therefore not altogether surprising that it would have been natural, likely even, for Anthony Emery to enter the Church, even if he was not ordained priest until he was 35 years old.

Mgr Leonard Emery was a priest in Coventry and subsequently rector of Oscott from 1935 until 1961, during which time his nephew was a student at the college. He believed that a rules-based system was the best way to run a seminary and likened his position to that of a monastic abbot, following the precept laid down in William Godfrey's *The Young Apostle* (1924), which taught: "Keep the rule and the rule will keep you." Emery oversaw the centenary celebrations of the college (on its present site) in 1938 and steered the seminary through the Second World War. Emery died in 1961, having celebrated the diamond jubilee of his priestly ordination and 25 years as college rector.

Bishop Humphrey Penderell Bright (1903–64) was born in Brentwood in Essex, studied at Oscott, and was ordained priest for the Diocese of Birmingham in 1928. During the Second World War, he served as a military chaplain and afterwards he was ordained titular Bishop of Soli, and auxiliary in Birmingham under (in the first instance) Archbishop Thomas Williams (1877–1946). Bishop Bright was a Father at the Second Vatican Council and died in 1964.

Turning now to Anthony Emery himself, he was born in Burton-on-Trent on 17 May 1918, the third of ten children. His father was Wilfrid

Ignatius Emery, who was an accountant, and his mother was Monica née Yeo. After school in Burton-on-Trent, Emery, like his father, began to study accountancy, but in 1940, he joined the Royal Army Service Corps which specialized in the supply and transport of military equipment: food, water, fuel, clothing, furniture and stationery. Emery most probably did his basic training at Aldershot, where the RASC then had its headquarters, and he saw action in Boulogne, although he narrowly escaped the terrible events at Dunkirk. During his time in the Army, he rose to the rank of major.

After being demobbed in 1945, he went to study at Campion House in Osterley in west London, a sort of "pre-seminary" and house of discernment run by the Jesuits, where basic Latin and biblical studies were taught to more mature candidates for the priesthood. Emery then went on to Oscott for a further six years. There was an upsurge in vocations to the priesthood after the war, and "the scholastic year 1947–1948 opened at Oscott with one hundred and nineteen attending classes in the college ... six years later in 1953 it is recorded that twenty-seven priests were ordained from the college."[2]

One of those was Anthony Emery, who was ordained priest at Oscott on 30 May 1953 by Bishop Humphrey Bright. The new priest served as curate for one year at St Brigid's in Northfield (Birmingham) and then went to St George's, Dorridge in Warwickshire. He served as chaplain to the local maternity hospital run by the Franciscan Missionary Sisters and became involved with Catholic education too. He is particularly remembered at the parish and school of Blessed Robert Grissold in Balsall Common near Coventry, where he was a regular visitor as a catechist, standing in for Mgr Tom Gavin on a Saturday morning. Later, when he became responsible for the diocese's schools, "he had to give up the Saturday morning instructions and a layperson took over".[3]

Father Emery served as deputy to the chairman of the Birmingham Archdiocesan Schools Commission, whom he succeeded in 1962, moving to Archbishop's House, Birmingham. It is said that Emery developed great skill in absorbing and explaining all the complexities of the education system, and he was also responsible for organizing a vast expansion in the provision of Catholic schools in the 1960s. He became a canon of Birmingham Cathedral Chapter in 1966, and in 1968 he succeeded Archbishop George Beck (1904–78) as chairman of the National Catholic Education Council.

On 4 December 1967, Emery was appointed titular Bishop of Tamallula and auxiliary bishop in Birmingham, and was ordained bishop on 4 March 1968 in St Chad's Cathedral by Archbishop George Dwyer (Birmingham), assisted by Bishop Edward Rudderham (Clifton) and Bishop Joseph Cleary (titular Bishop of Cresima and auxiliary in Birmingham). Bishop Emery was given responsibility for the counties of Oxfordshire, Warwickshire and Worcestershire.

One of the things that Bishop Emery did during this time was to bless and open the Church of Blessed Dominic Barberi at Littlemore (between Cowley and Iffley) in Oxfordshire in 1969. In and of itself, the opening of a modern church in the late 1960s would not be especially significant, but this striking church with its folded roof and unusual clerestory of glass pyramids is significant, for it commemorates the Italian Passionist priest Dominic Barberi, who received St John Henry Newman into the Church.

In 1822, Dr Newman, soon to become an Anglican cleric, was elected to a fellowship at Oriel College, Oxford. In 1827, the distinguished Provost of Oriel, Dr Edward Coplestone, was named as the Bishop of Llandaff, and Edward Hawkins, the vicar of St Mary's (Anglican) Church in Oxford was elected to succeed him. This vacancy at the University Church, under the patronage of Oriel College, was filled by the appointment of John Henry Newman, aged just 27. In addition to the responsibility for St Mary's, the post also carried the responsibility for the people of Littlemore which, as Newman later told his bishop, was one straggling street with neither church nor school and "scarcely a house beyond the rank of a cottage".

Newman threw himself into his work, developing great skill as a preacher at St Mary's. He wrote: "I preached my first University Sermon . . . it was to me like the feeling of spring weather after winter, and if I may so speak, I came out of my shell." Newman's sermons became legendary, and hundreds flocked to St Mary's to hear them. Alongside this high-profile work, Newman developed a pastoral sensitivity, ministering to the people of Littlemore. In particular, he raised funds and made plans so that a church could be built for them, the foundation stone of which was laid by Newman's mother on 21 July 1835.

At first, Newman remained resident at his rooms in Oriel and regularly travelled the three miles each way to Littlemore. Over time, he would spend more and more nights in Littlemore, travelling to Oxford when required. As Newman grew older, and the age gap between him and the students at Oriel grew too, he was more and more drawn to Littlemore, writing, "I am tempted to pitch my tent here." During Lent 1840, Newman left his curate in charge at St Mary's and spent the entire season in Littlemore practising austerities and devotions; a time that brought him great happiness.

Newman had plans to establish something of a "monastery" at Littlemore, but these came to nothing; notwithstanding he took the lease of an L-shaped row of stables which he had converted into a library, refectory and chapel with "dwelling-rooms" too. Keen to follow a more disciplined life, in April 1842, Newman moved out of Oriel and to the College, as it is now called, immersing himself in prayer and study. He resigned as Vicar of St Mary's the following year, preaching his last sermon there on 24 September. At the time, he was writing his book *An Essay on the Development of Christian Doctrine*, and initially it was his intention to complete the work and then decide whether it was the Anglican Church or the Roman Church which was the true inheritor of the faith of the Apostles and the Fathers, and consequentially whether he himself should "convert to Rome".

In the careful study for this book, and in the writing of it, Newman's mind was increasingly made up, and in the end, events overtook him. Newman's close friend J. D. Dalgairns travelled to Aston Hall in Staffordshire and was received into the Catholic Church on 29 September (Michaelmas) 1845 by the Passionist priest Dominic Barberi. While there, he suggested that Fr Barberi might visit Newman in Littlemore on his way to Belgium the following week.

Barberi arrived in Oxford on 8 October and was met by Dalgairns, who travelled with him to Littlemore, arriving by 10.30 p.m. The weather was atrocious, and the two men were soaked to the skin. (Incidentally, this evening journey is sometimes made as a "mini-pilgrimage" by faithful Catholics on the evening of 8 October, to this day.) While Fr Barberi's clothes were drying, Newman started his general confession, which he concluded the following day, and he was then received into full communion with the See of Peter on 9 October 1845. Newman remained in Littlemore until February 1846, when he left for good. Hence, as Bernard Bassett SJ has put it, "the name of a very small Oxfordshire village is known to thoughtful people around the world."[4]

In brief, Dominic Barberi was born near Viterbo in Italy on 22 June 1792. He entered the Passionist Order and became increasingly convinced that he should dedicate his ministry to working in England. With a faltering command of English, the Italian priest was at first ridiculed, but his reception of Newman into the Church made this hitherto obscure priest renowned. He contributed much to the conversion of England in the mid-nineteenth century and wrote a number of learned theological works. He died in Reading on 27 August 1849, and was beatified by Pope Paul VI, during the Second Vatican Council, on 27 October 1963. The cause for his canonization is underway.

Blessed Dominic Barberi is commemorated at the Church of Our Lady of Peace and Blessed Dominic Barberi at Earley, near Reading, and in Littlemore. Again briefly, Newman's College at Littlemore became for a time an almshouse in the possession of the (Anglican) Diocese of Oxford. It was put on the market by the diocese in 1951 and was acquired by the Fathers of the Birmingham Oratory. After nine years of uncertainty, the Fathers restored the College. Sisters of the Work live there now, caring for the College and receiving visitors and guests.

At this time, Littlemore became a parish in the Archdiocese of Birmingham with its own parish priest, and so a church was required to replace the scout hut where a Salesian priest from Cowley would regularly say Mass. The new church was designed by Peter Reynolds & Partners and built by Knowles & Son, and was blessed and opened by Bishop Emery on 3 May 1969.

After eight years as auxiliary, Bishop Emery was translated to the Diocese of Portsmouth. The announcement was made in September 1976, and Bishop Emery was installed in his new cathedral on St Martin's Day (11 November), by Mgr Sidney Mullarkey. It is said that Bishop Emery chose this feast as St Martin of Tours was also a soldier before he became a priest and a bishop.

Described as a day of "joy and colour", it saw some 300 priests, 24 bishops in full regalia, including the Apostolic Delegate, Archbishop

Bruno Heim in a scarlet *cappa magna*, and assorted civic dignitaries processing along Edinburgh Road, in a procession described as endless, and entering the cathedral. The canons greeted their new bishop and led him to his episcopal chair. A fanfare of trumpets resounded triumphantly through the cathedral and the congregation spontaneously burst into applause! Monks from Farnborough, Douai and Quarr chanted the Latin texts of the Mass, reinforced by boys from St Peter's School, Bournemouth. Mgr Sidney Mullarkey, the cathedral provost, presided over the proceedings lasting over two hours. Bishop Emery expressed his delight in the wonderful spirit of unity, harmony and goodwill he had found in the diocese, as evidenced by the many messages of welcome and the good wishes that he had received. He expressed his humility, conscious of his own limitations, but promised to strive to be worthy of the office of bishop.[5]

Bishop Emery took the motto *Sinite Parvulos Venire*, translated as "let the children come to me" (Matthew 19:14), clearly reflecting his educational priorities. Furthermore, it is said, Bishop Emery believed that this motto encapsulated the way that anyone, regardless of their age, should stand in their relationship with God.

Bishop Emery's first priority as bishop was to get to know his priests and to understand their needs, anxieties and pastoral concerns. He was well known for travelling widely across the diocese, visiting parishes and maintaining close contact with his priests.

His second priority, and in line with his motto, was the development of religious education and catechetics at all levels. Bishop Emery was particularly concerned that there should be some provision for adult religious education, and he established a Religious Education Council, appointing Mgr Patrick Murphy-O'Connor as episcopal vicar for religious education. Indeed, adult education and formation was his key strategy for renewal in the diocese.

Thirdly, he demonstrated his commitment to the missionary aspect of the work of the diocese, and the year after he was installed, he flew to Cameroon to visit his missionary clergy as the guest of the Bishop of Bamenda, at the time the Cameroonian Bishop (and later Archbishop) Paul Verdzekov. For three weeks, Bishop Emery "visited parishes, convents, out-stations, a diocesan seminary, meeting priests and people alike. Everywhere the welcome he received—in dance, songs and speeches—manifested the appreciation the African people had for their links with the Diocese of Portsmouth."[6] We may note in passing that over a forty-year period (from 1974 to 2014) over £1,000,000 had been raised for projects in Cameroon in the fields of faith, education and social welfare.

As discussed above, Bishop Emery's predecessor, now in Liverpool, convened the National Pastoral Congress. Emery engaged in local preparations for the congress and gave importance to the implementation of its recommendations, although he did not have the same enthusiasm for parish and deanery councils as his predecessor, and some of them began to fall into abeyance.

In 1981, Emery led the celebrations for the bicentenary of Bishop Challoner's death. Challoner was born in 1758 and was vice-president of Douai (in France) before joining the English missions in 1730. He was appointed coadjutor bishop to Bishop Petre of the London Vicariate (and titular Bishop of Debra) in 1741. Challoner succeeded Bishop Petre at his death and was the leading bishop in England of his day, guiding and expanding the Church despite the challenges of the times.

Bishop Emery celebrated Mass at the chapel at Milton Manor in Oxfordshire. The *Catholic Herald* columnist Patrick O'Donovan wrote:

> Bishop Challoner came here often although he did not seek out the rich. He left behind him here a Missal with his name on it and a poor and deeply moving chalice and a piece of the true cross given to him by some pope or other. There are some absolutely spiffing chasubles one of which Bishop Emery of Portsmouth wore for Mass.[7]

Also in 1981, Bishop Emery was somewhat unwillingly dragged into something of a controversy as reported in *The Times*, although Emery's behaviour was exemplary. In Wantage, the parish priest, Fr Wixted, incurred the displeasure of his bishop and the people, by celebrating a requiem for Bobby Sands (1954–81), a member of the Provisional Irish Republican Army. Sands had been convicted of helping to plan the bombing of the Balmoral Furniture Company in Dunmurry (1976), and died whilst on hunger strike at HM Prison Maze in Northern Ireland. As part of a wider article and carrying a photograph of Sands' burial, *The Times* newspaper reported:

> Father James Wixted, Roman Catholic parish priest of St John Vianney, Wantage, Oxfordshire who advertised a public Mass for Mr Sands was rebuked yesterday by his bishop, the Right Rev Anthony Emery. Four people attended the service last night, and about fifty gathered outside, many of them protestors. The half hour service was held behind locked doors.[8]

In order properly to understand the full significance of this event, some context is needed. Members of the Irish Republican Army (IRA) who were sent to prison were deemed to be criminals and terrorists by Irish Unionists and the British Government, but regarded as political prisoners by Republicans and sympathizers, who considered them to be waging a war. The prisoners sought a special "political status", and the headline issue was to be allowed to wear their own clothes (rather than prison uniform). Additionally, they demanded not to be obliged to work in the prison, to be able to associate more freely with other political prisoners and to have greater access to letters and parcels sent by mail.

The governments of the day denied the prisoners political status and various protests ensued. Tensions increased until a group of prisoners decided to deploy the "nuclear option" and went on hunger strike, believing this would force the government to give in. This caused a problem for the prime minister Margaret Thatcher and her Conservative government, for to give in to the prisoners would be a sign of weakness and would probably lead to further demands, but to hold firm would most likely lead to prisoner deaths and prisoners being regarded as "Republican martyrs". Secret negotiations were established via covert "back-channels" with the result that the prisoners were offered concessions and the initial hunger strikes were called off.

However, the prisoners subsequently felt that the government, or perhaps the prison service (there is uncertainty here), "fudged" the issues and reneged on their undertakings. A second wave of hunger strikes at the Maze Prison followed, led by Bobby Sands. During the hunger strike, there was a by-election in the constituency of Fermanagh and South Tyrone, and Bobby Sands (although in prison) stood as a candidate and was duly elected as a Westminster MP on the thirty-ninth day of his hunger strike. This was, of course a massive publicity coup for the strikers. On the sixty-sixth day of his hunger strike, on 5 May 1981, Bobby Sands died from starvation. He was the first of ten hunger strikers to die at that time. One hundred thousand people attended his funeral.

So for Fr Wixted to offer a Requiem Mass for Bobby Sands was not only a religious act but a highly charged political one too, and a definite "headache" for Bishop Emery. Moreover, it is historically significant to observe that Bobby Sands' election to the Westminster parliament was an important turning point for the Republican movement, for it enabled them to realize that they could pursue their aims through the ballot box alongside their "armed struggle".

Following the furore over Bobby Sands' Requiem Mass, it quickly became clear that Fr Wixted's time in Wantage had come to an end, and in May 1981 he left and returned to Ireland, settling near to where he had grown up. Fr Wixted died on 18 February 1998, and in a gracious act, Bishop Emery's successor, Bishop Crispian Hollis, celebrated a Requiem Mass for the repose of his soul in St John Vianney Church on 5 March 1998. The Mass was well attended, with parishioners staying for refreshments in the parish hall afterwards.

Bishop Emery was concerned for the future of the diocese and in particular for the provision of clergy. The number of new priests was not growing anything like as quickly as the Catholic population as a whole. Bishop Emery set up a Council for Priestly Vocation, to promote and administer applications for the priesthood. He also set up a Council for the Permanent Diaconate to facilitate the ordination of married men for service in the diocese. In the 1982 *Diocesan Year Book*, he wrote:

> For one hundred years there have been priests and religious sisters and brothers to serve Christ and his Church in our Diocese. Will there be in the future? The fields are ripe for the harvest but the labourers are now too few. The future depends on YOU. Please pray for vocations in our centenary year. Pray

> to the Lord of the Harvest to send more young men and women
> willing to give their lives in his service.

In 1982, Bishop Emery presided over the celebrations for the centenary of the diocese. He requested Fr Gerard Dwyer to write a history of the diocese; and as Fr Dwyer himself has written, were it not for his (Bishop Emery's) request, the *Diocese of Portsmouth Past and Present* would not have been written.

Bishop Emery also turned his attention to the cathedral and made further changes in the sanctuary. Originally the high altar was behind a wrought-iron screen. In 1906, Bishop Cahill brought the altar and baldacchino forward, raising them so that the congregation could see what the priest was doing at the altar. In 1971, Bishop Worlock ordered a reconfiguration after the Council: the baldacchino was demolished and a new altar was constructed and moved forward again. Altar rails and screens were removed. The priest faced the people so that priest and people celebrated together around the altar. In 1982, Bishop Emery raised the altar again on a further two steps.

The outside of the cathedral, the stone and the bricks, were cleaned and much of the interior redecorated. The area outside the west door was developed and the caretaker's lodge replaced by a new piazza. At the same time, the bishop's house was enlarged and the cathedral hall restored, all under the architect Mr John Wingfield and the cathedral administrator Canon Peter Doyle (*b.*1944), later Bishop Doyle of the Diocese of Northampton.

The formal celebrations of the centenary took place on 10 August 1982, the one hundredth anniversary of the opening of the cathedral, when Bishop Emery celebrated a Mass of thanksgiving in the cathedral, with over 100 clergy and the former bishop of the diocese, Archbishop Worlock. The congregation was chosen to represent the 180,000 Catholics in the diocese, and invitations were sent to every parish from Oxford and Berkshire to the Channel Islands. Bishop Emery said: "It is not individuals or buildings which are the Church. It is the living standards, priests, God and the people gathered around the bishop, who together are the temple where God lives in spirit. We are part of that." After the Mass, a reception and lunch were held in the cathedral grounds, and solemn vespers and benediction ended the day. The following year, on 2 May 1983, Cardinal Hume visited Portsmouth and celebrated another Mass of thanksgiving for the centenary of the diocese in Guildhall Square. In photographs, the Corinthian columns at the front of the late nineteenth-century neoclassical building, repaired and rebuilt after the Second World War, form a fitting and indeed splendid backdrop to the open-air altar.

Following the Second Vatican Council, liturgical changes were introduced, and Pope Paul VI promulgated the new order (*novus ordo*) of the Mass, to be said in the vernacular rather than in Latin, in 1969. The changes began to be implemented in 1970. Amongst those opposed to the changes, a number of societies and institutes were founded to treasure and maintain the celebration of Mass and other liturgical celebrations in the traditional Latin rite, sometimes called the *usus antiquor* or *vetus ordo*.

One such society was founded by Archbishop Marcel Lefebvre in 1970. Originally ordained as a diocesan priest, he joined the Holy Ghost Fathers for missionary work in Africa and was subsequently appointed titular Archbishop of Tulle. He was a conservative voice at the Second Vatican Council, and refused to implement the reforms within his community of which he was, by then, Superior General. In 1968, he resigned from the Holy Ghost Fathers and founded the priestly Society of Pius X (SSPX), a small community of priests and seminarians based at Ecône in Switzerland, with the permission of the local bishop. The society had the status of a pious union within the Church, and although there were tensions with Rome, the society continued to maintain its existence and mission.

In 1975, Lefebvre ordained four of his priests as bishops so that the work of the society could continue after his death (he was 81 at the time). However, without a mandate from Rome, and indeed against the clearly expressed wish of Pope John Paul II, Lefebvre and the four priests he had purported to ordain bishop were all excommunicated *latae sentetiae*, i.e. automatically and without further judicial process. These so-called "Ecône consecrations" put the society into further difficulties and an essentially schismatic relationship with Rome.

These details are relevant, because in 1988, SSPX opened a house in Portsmouth, converting a disused branch of Lloyds Bank at 14 Kingston Road, Fratton into the Church of Our Lady Help of Christians. This incurred the displeasure of Bishop Anthony Emery, who was said to "disapprove", but, in reality, there was nothing he could do about it. As a coda, we may note that the church in Fratton was closed and the building sold to help fund the new and expanding SSPX school (and church) of St Michael in Burghclere (in Hampshire), originally founded in 1991.

Bishop Emery died suddenly and unexpectedly on 5 April 1988 (aged 69). He had gone to bed feeling unwell and was discovered dead the following day.

His funeral took place nine days later in Portsmouth Cathedral, which was packed full; the newspaper observed mourners were "crammed into every available space". As Metropolitan, it fell to Michael Bowen, the Archbishop of Southwark, to lead the requiem, but he was unwell and in the event Cardinal Basil Hume OSB presided. Some 200 priests from Portsmouth and Birmingham dioceses attended along with 30 bishops, local naval and civic dignitaries and family members. Proceedings nearly went awry on the day before the funeral, when the pavement outside the cathedral, along which the bishops were to process, was dug up by workmen! But disaster was averted when the workmen agreed to relay the pavement before the noon Mass.

Bishop Joseph Cleary, the senior auxiliary bishop in Birmingham, paid tribute to Bishop Emery, noting his experience, wide knowledge of, and contribution to, Catholic education. He also said: "Whenever I thought of a gentleman I thought of Bishop Emery. Nothing was too much for him in the way of being helpful, considerate and kind to the people he met."[9] Cleary said that Bishop Emery rarely talked and never boasted about his achievements but just got on with the job.

Archbishop Worlock paid tribute to his fellow bishop:

> I am deeply saddened to hear of the sudden death of Bishop Emery. Naturally he will be greatly missed as an outstanding educationalist and as a stalwart promoter of Catholic schools. But he was also a much respected bishop, loved by priests and the

people of Portsmouth. His unassuming style could never disguise his pastoral abilities and his leadership as a bishop.

It was said that he had the valuable trio of charm, humility and sharpness of mind. A Catholic spokesman wrote:

> Above all he was a much loved father and shepherd to the people, religious community and priests of the diocese who expressed their love and affection at a Mass of Thanksgiving, on the tenth anniversary of his installation in the cathedral. The sadness of Emery's sudden death was mingled with gratitude for such a good and faithful pastor and minister of God's word and sacraments.[10]

Bishop Emery was buried in Milton Cemetery in Portsmouth.

Notes

1   Cf. Michael E. Williams, *Oscott College in the Twentieth Century* (Leominster: Gracewing, 2001), p. 71, n. 7.

2   Ibid., p. 98.

3   See< http://www.brgparish.org.uk/archive/history/index.php>, accessed 30 August 2024.

4   For this and much of the information above, cf. Bernard Basset, *Newman at Littlemore*, published by the Friends of Newman.

5   Cf. *Portsmouth News*, 11 November 1976.

6   Gerard Dwyer, *Diocese of Portsmouth: Past and Present* (Portsmouth: Portsmouth Diocesan Centenary Committee, 1981), p. 131.

7   Quoted in Dwyer, *Diocese of Portsmouth: Past and Present*, p. 19.

8   *The Times*, 8 May 1981.

9   *Portsmouth News*, 14 April 1988.

10   Cf. *Portsmouth News*, 5 April 1988.

Roger Francis Crispian Hollis (1989–2012)

Crispian Hollis was born in Bristol on 17 November 1936, the son of converts to Catholicism. His father was Christopher Hollis (1902–77), who was educated at Eton and Balliol. He was a schoolmaster, author and Conservative Member of Parliament for Devizes, from 1945–55. Also a friend of Ronald Knox and Evelyn Waugh, he converted to Catholicism in 1924. Crispian's mother was Madeleine née King. Young Crispian had two brothers and a sister. There were notable churchmen in his family: his paternal grandfather was Bishop George Arthur Hollis, Anglican Suffragan Bishop of Taunton, and his uncle was Arthur Michael Hollis, the Anglican Bishop of Madras in south India between 1942 and 1954.

Additionally, Sir Roger Henry Hollis (1905–73), after whom Crispian was probably named and on whose account he was called Crispian, was his father's brother and an intelligence officer who worked for MI5. Having served in Hong Kong and Shanghai, he was Director General of MI5 from 1956 until 1965. There were some suspicions that Hollis was a double agent, really working for the Russians, though he always denied these allegations, and subsequent investigations have tended to exonerate him. After his retirement, Sir Roger moved to Tasmania, Australia and wrote an account of his life called *Spycatcher*, which sold over two million copies.

Crispian Hollis was born prematurely and was baptized within a couple of days of his birth. He went to school at Stonyhurst College, the Jesuit school in Lancashire founded in 1593, where his father had once been on the staff. Indeed, young Crispian was taught by Thomas Holt who had previously been one of his father's pupils. Although co-educational now, after the war the school only admitted boys, but there were increasing numbers of lay teaching staff; also the seminary known as St Mary's Hall, at one time on the same site, had moved to Heythrop Hall. Hollis received the sacrament of confirmation at school, although he recalled that, "I do not remember any concerted preparation—but then I was at a boarding school; the ceremony was celebrated without Mass because it was in the afternoon and this was the time before evening Masses were allowed. The ceremony was in Latin, the bishop was remote and seemed rather grumpy."[1] Hollis discovered cricket at school and was an enthusiastic player, indeed his ambition at that time was to play cricket for Somerset.

After school, Hollis undertook his national service with the Somerset Light Infantry (also known as Prince Albert's). Most probably, he would have done his ten weeks of basic training at the Light Infantry Training Centre at Cove, near Aldershot, where (from 1948) all light infantrymen were trained. Hollis joined up alongside Cuthbert ROM and Symon RHC and all three were appointed Second Lieutenant on 7 May 1955.

The main task of the Somerset Light Infantry was in Malaya, the "Malaya Emergency", as it was known, battling the Communist Malayan Races Liberation Army. Described as little more than bandits, they were a guerrilla army who were well armed and trained and lived in the jungle. Hence, most of the Army's operations took place southwest of Kuala Lumpur, in a jungle environment, and then later to the east of the city. There were swamps too: called the north swamp, the south swamp and the mangrove swamp, covering some 1,000 square miles. In the swamps, "sluggish brown and crocodile infested rivers flowed through a foul morass, where a man might wade all day in the thick liquid up to his knees, thighs or even waist."[2] It is said that tigers, elephants and snakes were not, as might be expected, the greatest natural danger, but rather mosquitoes, ants and hornets—the fiercest in the world.

Hollis completed his military service in 1956 but remained registered with the regiment as an Army Emergency Reserve Officer, which would have probably involved an annual training camp, and he appeared in the Army List until 1960. In 1959, the regiment amalgamated with the Duke of Cornwall's Light Infantry to form the Cornwall and Somerset Light Infantry. Hollis was promoted to Lieutenant on 11 January 1957, and by 1960 he was the third senior Lieutenant in the unit by date of appointment.

After his military service, Hollis went up to Balliol College in Oxford in 1956. Balliol is distinguished as one of the very oldest Oxford colleges, founded in the thirteenth century. Depending on how you understand the establishment of a college, it has a claim to be the oldest college in Oxford and in the English-speaking world. It is also renowned for having produced (at the time of writing) 12 Nobel Prize laureates and four British prime ministers, not to mention a host of other scholars and public figures.

Hollis read modern history and continued to play cricket seriously. It is worth pausing here to note that Hollis is the only Bishop of Portsmouth to hold an Oxford degree, and indeed more generally, an Oxford (or a Cambridge) degree is a rare thing amongst the Catholic hierarchy, although there are, of course, notable exceptions. Following the Reformation until 1871, Roman Catholics were effectively barred from Oxford, since admission (matriculation) required an individual to swear an oath to the monarch and the established Church. In 1854, the requirement of allegiance to the Church of England was lifted, except for theology students, although many Oxford colleges retained their barriers. It was not until the Test Act of 1871 that Parliament opened the doors of the universities of Oxford, Cambridge and Durham to students of all faiths and none.

Understandably therefore, Catholics had traditionally looked to the Continent for appropriate higher-level education. In 1845, the former student at Trinity College, later Fellow at Oriel and Anglican cleric John Henry (later Cardinal) Newman converted to Catholicism. In 1851, Sir John Simeon the Anglican MP for the Isle of Wight resigned his seat and was also received into the Catholic Church, although he was re-elected to parliament in 1865.

Simeon became involved in the debate about whether Catholics should send their sons to the English universities of the day. "The prevailing ecclesiastical view was that attendance at the old universities could not be justified",[3] although the English bishops preferred to caution against attendance rather than issue an outright ban. Simeon became involved with other notable Catholics, particularly other recent converts, and observed that it was impossible for the Catholic Body in England to elevate themselves into intellectual equality with their fellow citizens unless something was done to improve their education, but he feared that "Old Catholics" (i.e. non-converts) would see no necessity for change.

The discussion of this question brought Simeon into contact with Newman who, between 1854 and 1857, had been rector of the Catholic University in Dublin. Simeon, with other influential laymen, drew up a document which was sent to the *Propaganda Fide* in Rome, but the bishops were instructed to advise against attendance at the English universities. Hence, even after 1871, it was relatively rare for Catholics, including would-be clerics, to take advantage of the educational opportunities at Oxford and Cambridge. The University of London, founded in 1836 on a largely secular model, tended to be preferred. Hollis was an unusual case, although it is clear that in one sense he was simply following in the footsteps of his father.

At Oxford, Hollis discerned a vocation to the priesthood, although the idea had first entered his mind while he was at school. He has said that there was no blinding light but rather a persistent voice—a calling that had, at least, to be tested. He has described his vocation in this way: "The call to the priesthood, even though one's consciousness of it may take a long time to develop is for me and for the future of my life. It is specifically what God has called me to do. It is not a generic calling, but intensely personal."[4]

After Oxford, Hollis went, in 1959, to Rome to study at the Venerable English College. The whole college had been exiled in England during the Second World War and had only returned to Rome, a city scarred by bombing, in 1946. By 1959, Mgr Gerard ("Jock") Tickle was the rector; he was a no-nonsense, affable and even-tempered man. He had been a chaplain to the forces during the war and had many practical skills, such as painting, cooking and even plumbing and bricklaying, and he did much to improve the college and the villa at Palazzola. He bought second-hand furniture to equip additional rooms for students and visitors. Mgr Tickle also had good "man-management skills"; he had the support of the students and was also able to deal with Roman officialdom in a measured, polite but determined way. He also had a reputation as a superb host, which he rather had to be as the college accommodated many guests during the Second Vatican Council, which took place at that time (1962–5).

Hollis was ordained to the priesthood, for the Diocese of Clifton, on 11 July 1965 in the College's chapel at the Villa Palazzola by William Cardinal Heard, at that time Dean of the Roman Rota and titular bishop of Feradi Maius. He has recalled: "I was ordained by an aged Scottish cardinal who was, as it were, swathed in purple (or at least scarlet) and fine linen. He vested at the altar, he wore buskins and gloves, there was no homily and the ceremony was conducted entirely in Latin." Hollis stayed on in Rome and completed a Licence in Theology (STL) in 1966. He then returned to England and served a brief curacy at Christ the King, Amesbury in Wiltshire.

Then, in 1967, he moved to Oxford as assistant Catholic chaplain to the university, working under Fr Michael Hollings, who influenced him greatly. He lived and worked at the Old Palace in St Aldates, which has housed the Catholic chaplaincy since 1920. Originally two houses, the Old Palace is believed to be so named because the first (Anglican) Bishop of Oxford, Robert King, may have lived there. The facade was reconstructed in the 1950s, and in 1969 Fr Hollings commissioned the architects Ahrends, Burton & Koralek to develop the site adjoining the Old Palace. This new versatile chaplaincy building opened in 1972 and contains the chapel, the library, the Newman Room for meetings and some student accommodation. Later, in due course, Hollings moved on and Hollis succeeded him as Catholic chaplain to the university, where he remained until 1977.

Terms at Oxford are very short—just eight weeks—and the pace of life is very fast and frenetic. Hollis described it as a busy time celebrating the sacraments and offering pastoral support to the students. The chaplaincy opened at 6.30 a.m. and closed at midnight, and the chaplain could be on the go all day. Having said this, there was a strong sense of community centred on the Eucharist, although Fr Hollis also recalled that there was an open-door policy at the chaplaincy and there was no space that one could securely call one's own.

It was while Fr Hollis was chaplain at Oxford that he made his first trip to Lourdes on the University Pilgrimage. After the first trip in 1967, he went annually with them until 1981, developing a great affection for, and attachment to, the place, which continued when Hollis went to Clifton and then to Portsmouth. He has led joint diocesan pilgrimages to Lourdes and was a patron of the Catholic Association Hospitalité until 2011.

In 1977, Hollis was appointed as Catholic Assistant to the Head of Religious Broadcasting at the BBC. He has written:

> In practice I was a producer for Radios 2, 3 and 4, with slots like 'Prayer for the Day' being my responsibility. I was also responsible for the placing and production of all RC outside broadcasts, and a source of advice for the Head of Religious Broadcasting. My work was mainly with radio though I had commentary and advisory work with the TV services, especially during the year of the three popes (1978) and John Paul II's visit to Ireland.

This work began a lifetime of involvement with the media, where he honed his considerable communication skills. One might not always agree with Hollis' message, but he delivered it with clarity and eloquence.

In 1981, Hollis was appointed administrator of the cathedral at Clifton and vicar general of the diocese, under Bishop Mervyn Alexander, with special responsibility for ecumenical affairs. It was his first real parish appointment, and he recalls it as a happy time. He had a good rapport with his parishioners and fellow priests, and he thrived, particularly having "come home" to the diocese for which he had been ordained. At this time, he also became a member of the Independent Broadcasting Authority (IBA), a panel of religious advisors, and he joined CRAC, the Central Religious Advisory Committee for the BBC and the IBA.

Just six years later in 1987, Hollis was appointed auxiliary bishop in Birmingham under Archbishop Maurice Couve de Murville. The appointment was announced on 13 February 1987, and Hollis was ordained titular Bishop of Cincari and auxiliary in Birmingham on 5 May 1987 in St Chad's Cathedral, Birmingham, by Archbishop Couve de Murville (Birmingham) assisted by Bishop Joseph Gray (Shrewsbury) and Bishop Mervyn Alexander (Clifton).

Bishop Hollis was given special responsibility for the part of Oxfordshire (north of the Thames) that lies in the Archdiocese of

Birmingham, but he had little time to settle into this new role, because just 18 months later he was appointed Bishop of Portsmouth, on 6 December 1988. He was installed in his new cathedral on 27 January 1989. There were nearly 1,000 guests packed into the cathedral as Archbishop Michael Bowen of the Southwark Archdiocese installed Bishop Hollis. Cardinal Basil Hume was also in attendance, as was the papal representative Archbishop Luigi Barbarito. Bishop Hollis promised to "guide and serve" the people of Portsmouth.

Bishop Hollis took as his episcopal motto *Per Ducatum Evangelii* meaning literally "by the leading of the gospel" or "under the guidance of the gospel". Although this is surely a good motto for any Christian, it is a quotation from the prologue of the sixth-century Rule of St Benedict:

> Let us therefore make for ourselves a girdle out of faith and perseverance in good works, and under the guidance of the Gospel let us pursue our way in his paths, so that we may deserve to see him who has called us to his kingdom.[5]

In 1999, Pope Saint John Paul II would write to the Benedictine Order on the occasion of the 1,500th anniversary of its founding. He wrote:

> I was delighted to learn that the great Benedictine monastic family intends to celebrate the 1,500th anniversary of St Benedict's foundation in Subiaco of that 'scola dominici servitii' which down the centuries led countless numbers of men and women 'per ducatum evangelii' to a closer union with Christ.[6]

Bishop Hollis established himself in Bishop's House with Fr John Nelson (later monsignor and vicar general) as his first secretary, chancellor and master of ceremonies. He had a structured routine, beginning with an hour of prayer in his chapel each morning and centred on the daily celebration of the Eucharist. He has been described as a man of deep prayer. Bishop Hollis also observed that when he moved from Birmingham to Portsmouth, he knew few of the priests and hardly any of the people. His response to this daunting prospect, the realization that as diocesan bishop, rather than auxiliary, the buck stopped with him, was to pray and to do his best.

His first years as bishop were busy ones, getting to know his diocese and his clergy. He made parish visitations and travelled for confirmations, he chaired the board of trustees, and was involved with the governance of the diocese and with other bishops in the bishops' conference. Fr John Nelson recalled that there was "a lot of travelling around, a lot of doing engagements, school visits, confirmations, being at things. It was not unusual to do 3 or 4 engagements and 200 miles in a day."[7]

By 2002, the tyranny of the diary, as Bishop Hollis called it, was beginning to wear him down, and the morale of the diocese was threatened by a diocesan priest who had been jailed for downloading child pornography. The cathedral chapter urged Bishop Crispian to have a proper rest, and he took a three-month sabbatical between August and October 2003. He spent a month with his sister, a month in France, and a month absolutely on his own in his sister's holiday home in Cornwall. He has said that the solitary month was most important and that it revived him and prepared him for his ongoing episcopal ministry. The tiredness slipped away, and Bishop Hollis was aware of the Lord's presence and again attuned to the deeply personal nature of his calling. He now had a new impetus and the courage and confidence to lead the diocese forward.

He remarked that for a number of years he had felt that neither he nor the diocese could simply continue in the old ways. Congregations were diminishing in number as were priests. He finally realized that just hoping that things would improve was not sufficient. It was not so much that he or the diocese had been doing things badly or getting things wrong, but rather that the context in which the Church had to work had changed. Playing to his own strengths he realized that a new kind of communication was required: a new model of church and of ministry. The watchwords of this new model were communion and mission.

In 2004, Bishop Hollis communicated his new vision, his plan for the development of the diocese in a document *Growing Together in Christ*, which explained his nascent pastoral strategy: not one that he would impose, but one that came from priests and people working and praying together. Bishop Hollis' vision was very much a "bottom-up" rather than a "top-down" operation. Importantly, people felt that the bishop had invited them to contribute: to express their needs and concerns and that he had listened. The people felt involved, that they had some input into, and ownership of, the process and thus they were more positively inclined to follow his lead. To put this another way, Bishop Hollis wisely distinguished between power and authority, recognizing that there was little point instructing people to do what made them unhappy, rather it was preferable to share his vision and take people along with him.

In the summer of 2005, a Diocesan Pastoral Assembly was held in Reading, which produced a new diocesan pastoral plan and the document *Go Out and Bear Fruit*, encouraging collaborative ministry between clergy and laity based on communion and mission. The document had two key elements. The first was that the Sunday Mass should be the heart of every Catholic community, truly the source and summit of Catholic life. The second element was the establishment of Pastoral Areas, groups of parishes which could work together to achieve things they could not achieve individually, for example the funding of a youth worker. Part of the plan was to share the dwindling number of priests so that the Sunday Mass would be available to as many people as possible. Additionally, the Diocesan Pastoral Council offered support to pastoral areas and parishes, created networks between those working in similar areas, led courses relevant to parish life, offered support in faith development and encouraged collaboration and the sharing of resources. This collaborative approach was radical if not revolutionary, but Bishop Hollis also recognized that his plans were not set in stone but would have to change and evolve over time.

Bishop Peter Doyle (Northampton), who was a priest in the diocese at the time, has written that at first he was baffled by what Bishop Hollis was trying to do, but that over time he came to recognize that Bishop Hollis wanted his people to develop and mature in faith; for each person to recognize and accept their role in the Church, based on their baptism, and to be a true herald of the gospel. Canon Doyle, who administered the diocese when Bishop Hollis was on sabbatical, wrote: "Bishop Crispian opened up a broader vision of the Church and the part each of us is called to play in building up the Kingdom of God."[8]

Sometimes it is said or written that in 2004 Bishop Hollis founded Holy Trinity monastery in East Hendred, Oxfordshire, as a Benedictine house of contemplative nuns. More accurately, in September 2004, Bishop Hollis welcomed a new, small group of Benedictine contemplative religious sisters to the diocese who established a convent in the presbytery at East Hendred. Originally from Stanbrook Abbey in Worcestershire, three nuns broke away to create a more innovative form of community, dedicated to spiritual outreach and the use of new media and technology.

The dynamic Dame Catherine Wybourne OSB (1954–2022), also known as "Digitalnun", studied history at Cambridge, completed a PhD in Spain and worked for a time in banking before entering the convent at Stanbrook. She became increasingly convinced that new technology, primarily the internet and social media, could be utilized to spread the Christian message, particularly as it pertained to monasticism and the Rule of Saint Benedict. She once described the computer as the "modern scriptorium".

She left Stanbrook along with Dame Lucy ("Quietnun") and Dame Teresa, and the new community became an autonomous convent of diocesan right sanctioned by Bishop Hollis, rather than universally recognized by the papacy. Sister Catherine wrote a regular column for *The Universe* newspaper, and she developed the community's website. The sisters also made audio books for blind and visually impaired people and ran an audio book library. In 2009, the sisters won the Premier Christian Media People's Award for their work. In late May 2012, the community relocated to Howton Grove Priory, a barn conversion in Herefordshire and part of the Archdiocese of Cardiff. Dame Catherine died from cancer in 2022.

Bishop Crispian took ecumenism seriously and was a founder member of Churches Together in Hampshire, now known as Churches Together in Hampshire and the Isle of Wight. Following the Swanwick conference of 1987, there was a transition from a "Council of Churches" to a "Churches Together" model, and CTE, Churches Together in England, was founded in 1990. The vision was to create a space where collaboration and mutual understanding could grow. Bishop Hollis also worked closely with the Anglican Bishop of Winchester and the Anglican Bishop of Portsmouth.

In June 2009, Bishop Hollis (then aged 72) launched the diocesan *Living our Faith* Campaign, aimed at putting the diocese on a firm financial footing. People were not only encouraged to give money but to pledge money, that is to commit to regular giving. In June 2010, the campaign finished with over £13,000,000 having been pledged—a remarkable achievement and a credit to Bishop Hollis. In the 2019 report of the diocesan trustees, it was stated that "no significant further increase is expected", and the report also outlined how some of the funds had been spent under four separate headings: clergy training and support, parish and pastoral area lay formation, renewing facilities and finally parish local funds. In 2014, the trustees approved a follow-up campaign to seek continued financial support from existing donors and support from those who had not yet given, called *Our Parishes' Future*. A further fundraising campaign, entitled *Closer to Christ*, was launched in 2023.

Also in 2009, there was a visit to the UK of the relics of the French Carmelite nun Saint Thérèse of Lisieux, and Portsmouth was the first port of call. Catholics from across the region and beyond assembled at the cathedral, and Bishop Hollis welcomed them and the relics before celebrating the Mass, greeting school groups who visited and leading an all-night prayer vigil. There was a special invitation to the sick, and Bishop Hollis anointed them at his Mass.

As part of the Catholic Bishops' Conference of England and Wales, Hollis had a national role in the fields of communication, education and European affairs. He is particularly remembered as an excellent communicator; he remembered people once he had met them, and he had impeccable manners. He was urbane and knew what it was to be a bishop. He served as chairman of the Catholic Media Trust and chairman of the Bishops' Committee for Europe. He also spoke more widely on behalf of the bishops and (for example) responded to the earthquake in Haiti in 2010 with a moving and compassionate statement:

> The news from Haiti is heartbreaking. The loss of life, the destruction of buildings and the whole fabric of civic life—all are devastating features of the burdens now having to be borne by survivors.
>
> I offer my heartfelt prayers and those of the whole diocese of Portsmouth to the people of Haiti. I promise that together with CAFOD we will do all we can to help.

> I am praying particularly for those who have died and their families which are suffering such sad bereavement. In a special way I will be remembering my brother bishop, Archbishop Serge Miot, who is said to be among those who have died.[9]

A more light-hearted perspective of Bishop Hollis is again provided in a little vignette by Cormac Murphy-O'Connor in his memoir *An English Spring*. In 1990, Murphy-O'Connor was Bishop of Arundel and Brighton, which was celebrating the silver jubilee of its establishment that year (A&B was separated from the Archdiocese of Southwark in 1965). Murphy-O'Connor relates that in a characteristically Sussex way, after the solemn Mass there was a picnic for several thousand people and a cricket match. The Bishop's XI lined up against the Duke of Norfolk's XI:

> There was great applause when I walked out to open the batting with Michael Bowen the previous bishop of the diocese. I would like to be able to say that we marked the occasion with a half-century opening stand, but Micky and I were both out within a couple of overs. But it was a great occasion with a strong innings from Crispian Hollis, Bishop of Portsmouth.[10]

Here we see that Hollis was a capable cricketer, no doubt something of a sportsman all round and a "good sport" too, joining in with the celebrations.

In January 2010, Bishop Hollis made an *ad limina* visit to Rome, along with Archbishop Vincent Nichols and six other bishops. This was the first visit by English and Welsh bishops since the election of Pope Benedict XVI. These visits are usually every five years (quinquennial), and the bishops travel *ad limina apostolorum*, to the threshold of the apostles to venerate the tombs of St Peter and St Paul, thereby implicitly accepting the pope as St Peter's successor, the universal pastor of the Church. The bishops traditionally meet the pope collectively and individually, to give an account of their dioceses.

Much of the discussion at that visit was about the shortage of priestly vocations. Bishop Kieran Conry, then bishop of Arundel and Brighton, revealed that the English and Welsh bishops' report had "made clear that we are facing challenges that the Church in the west is generally facing. These include a more strident secularism and atheism alongside a declining number of priests which is having an effect on parish life." John Rawsthorne, then Bishop of Hallam, also emphasized during the visit that a shortage of priests would be a key issue, and he reported the bishops' wish to consult with the pope on the matter.

Also during the 2010 *ad limina* visit and in the light at that time of the imminent beatification of (now Saint) John Henry Newman, the English and Welsh bishops asked to visit the places especially connected with the life of the cardinal. They visited the Chapel of the Three Kings, now inside the Missio headquarters but at the time the chapel of the *Collegio di Propaganda Fide*, where Newman had been ordained priest by Cardinal Giacomo Filippo Fransoni on 30 May 1847. They also visited the Newman Chapel in the same building where Newman first celebrated Mass, on the following Thursday, the feast of *Corpus Christi*. In Newman's time, this was the Jesuits' chapel, and Newman offered the Mass on an altar above the shrine of St Hyacinth, not far from his room. This altar, which had been moved to the new *Collegio Urbano* on the *Gianicolo*, was recently returned to *Propaganda Fide* and placed in a chapel now dedicated to Newman.[11]

Of course, it was later that same year that Pope Benedict XVI made a state visit to the United Kingdom. The principal event was the beatification of Cardinal John Henry Newman in Cofton Park, Birmingham on Sunday 19 September 2010. The pope could have delegated this task to somebody else, but on account of his great admiration, and indeed affection, for the work of Newman, Pope Benedict undertook the task himself. The official announcement of the state visit recorded:

> Since the election of Pope Benedict XVI, in April 2005, all Beatification ceremonies, with a few exceptions in Rome, had been held in the diocese where the servant of God was either born, lived or died. It was the personal wish of Pope Benedict XVI to come to England to beatify Cardinal Newman in the Archdiocese of Birmingham.[12]

In November 2009, Pope Benedict promulgated the Apostolic Constitution *Anglicanorum coetibus*, which (as the name suggests) allows for groups of Anglicans to be received into the Roman Catholic Church in a corporate way. The accompanying "Complementary Norms" allowed for the establishment of personal ordinariates led by an ordinary at its head. At present, there are three: of Our Lady of Walsingham in England and Wales (and in Scotland by extension), of the Chair of St Peter in the US, and of the Southern Cross in Australia. Membership is personal rather than on a geographical basis, and in law an ordinariate is juridically comparable to a diocese. Moreover, the ordinariates are permitted to use liturgical books, known collectively as Divine Worship, approved by the Holy See, which maintain the distinct liturgical and pastoral patrimony of the Anglican Communion.

Amongst the English and Welsh bishops, there was something of a mixed reaction to *Anglicanorum coetibus* and the establishment of the Ordinariate. In 2010, Bishop Alan Hopes, himself a convert, was appointed as the episcopal delegate of the CBCEW (Catholic Bishops' Conference of England and Wales) for the implementation of *Anglicanorum coetibus*, although it is said that he did so with limited enthusiasm. Additionally, it may be noted that during Pope Benedict's 2010 visit, he met with the bishops of England, Scotland and Wales at St Mary's College, Oscott, and in his address to them, he urged them to use the new translation of the Missal (2010) for a renewed in-depth catechesis on the Eucharist; and he also urged them to be generous in the implementation of *Anglicanorum coetibus*. Pope Benedict asked the bishops to see the constitution as a prophetic gesture, reminding them that the quest for visible unity in the Church remains an imperative and not an option.

Like Bishop Hopes, I think it is fair to say that Bishop Hollis was similarly lukewarm at first, but over time he changed his mind and became more supportive. In a pastoral letter dated 7 March 2011, Bishop Hollis admitted that he had had his "own misgivings and questions about the development of the ordinariate, but [wrote] I have now come to see this as a unique moment and I welcome warmly those who are joining us".[13]

In May 2011, Bishop Hollis ordained three former Anglican clergy, living within the geographical bounds of the Catholic Diocese of

Portsmouth to the diaconate in a low-key celebration in the Chapel of St John in the cathedral. Then on 25 June of the same year he ordained the same three men to the priesthood in the main body of the church. It is recalled by one of the men ordained, that Bishop Hollis made hospitable and supportive comments about the wives of the two married men.

In addition to these 2011 ordinations, Bishop Hollis has ordained a number of other former Anglicans to the priesthood (including Edwin Barnes, one-time principal of St Stephen's House, Oxford and former Anglican Bishop of Richborough), and it has been reported that he expressed a real sense of joy at the ordinations, tempered with an equally impressive level of respect for the ministry of the candidates in the Church of England.

On 19 November 2011, a special Mass was celebrated for Bishop Hollis' seventy-fifth birthday and in thanksgiving for his 22 years as a bishop. Mgr Nicholas France preached the homily, emphasizing that it was not a funeral and he was not preaching a panegyric. Mgr France characterized the Hollis years as both consolidation and development in many areas of diocesan life. He noted the development of Catholic education and the missionary outreach overseas and in the twinned diocese of Bamenda. He characterized Bishop Hollis as a good administrator, financially acute, creating "over the years an excellent department for finance and church property and an able body of diocesan trustees".[14] It is said that he particularly loathed inefficiency and couldn't put up with it, but that he was also fair and honest. He would always try to put the best gloss on any particular situation and would, wherever possible, give his priests and people the benefit of the doubt.

At the end of 2011, having reached his seventy-fifth birthday and having undergone surgery for bowel cancer (diagnosed the year before), Bishop Hollis tendered his resignation to Rome, and the following July it was accepted, as Hollis' successor was announced. Unusually, but perhaps understandably, given Hollis' age and health, there was some disquiet about the amount of time the Vatican took to appoint a successor, with one observer commenting that "it is frankly cruel to require any priest or bishop to continue in office to the age of 75, but when someone is not in the best of health it is shameful to keep them in office".[15]

Having said that, I have it on reliable authority and independently corroborated that an appointment was made but the appointee (for reasons unknown to me) declined the offer. Again I have heard the rumour that he accepted at first and then subsequently declined, and hence the apparent "delay" becomes much more understandable. Furthermore, the possibility exists that more than one person may have been invited to take up the position and declined.

I think two observations can be usefully made. The first is particular: to suggest that the Vatican was somehow "cruel" in its dealings with Hollis' resignation is surely not accurate. We can suppose that the Apostolic Nuncio and the Holy See acted in a timely way, but that there were problems or at least complications which slowed the process down. The second point is more general, and I address it to myself as much as anyone else: when writing about priests and bishops, and public figures more generally, it is important to remember that one doesn't always know the full story and some details remain confidential. Hence value judgements about particular events, and historical events especially, must be made with a good deal of caution and circumspection, and care must be taken to guard against over-hasty judgements.

On 31 May 2012, Bishop Hollis celebrated a farewell Mass with his clergy in Basingstoke. He said to the clergy that his years as a bishop had been immeasurably good, and he thanked them for their unselfish commitment, faith, support and cooperation. He observed that his successor would,

> inherit, in financial terms, a not inconsiderable war chest. He will inherit a restructured diocese with which to face some of the challenges to the mission and life of the Church in the 21st century. Most importantly he will inherit a body of clergy who know how to work collaboratively and are ready to take full responsibility for the task of proclaiming and living the Gospel.[16]

Bishop Hollis retired to the Somerset village of Mells, in the area that had been his childhood home. His plan was to assist in the Clifton Diocese as a supply priest and help in any other way that he could. He declared that he was among friends and that he was content, and it was observed that he had achieved a great deal, not least on a personal level, and a real serenity.

As a mark of respect and indeed affection for the man who had been Bishop of Portsmouth for 22 years the section of Edinburgh Road outside the cathedral was renamed Bishop Crispian Way. Bishop Hollis said:

> I am overwhelmed by the honour that is being done to me by the renaming of what I might call our section of Edinburgh Road. As far as I know, no such honour has been done to any of my predecessors and I am still at a bit of a loss to know what I have done to deserve this honour.

Some years earlier the Friends of Portsmouth Cathedral commissioned the painter Pierre Bamin, who has painted a number of bishops including Bishop Emery, to paint Bishop Crispian and the painting, completed in 2007, is striking. The paintings hang in Bishop's House:

> Bishop Anthony Emery now hangs to the left of Bishop Hollis' portrait ... both flanking a doorway to the main halls, both mirroring each other. Emery stands at the back of the cathedral, Hollis to the front. The crucifix that hangs at the rear of the cathedral in Bishop Hollis' painting is the same cross that features above the altar in Bishop Emery's. Little details like this are easy to miss but add depth to a painting once they are discovered.[17]

To sum up, Bishop Hollis has led a remarkably full and active life. He was rooted in an academic tradition at Balliol and in Rome, he served in the army and as a university chaplain. But as a bishop he was forward-looking and innovative. He had a vision and did much to implement it, not by imposing but by collaboration and encouragement. One priest said to me that Bishop Crispian had his critics and his natural patrician style was sometimes misunderstood, but it was universally agreed that he was a good bishop.

Notes

1   *Portsmouth People*, December 2012, p. 3.

2   Kenneth Whitehead, *History of the Somerset Light Infantry* (Somerset Light Infantry, 1961), p. 35.

3   Paul Shrimpton, *A Catholic Eton? Newman's Oratory School* (Leominster: Gracewing 2005), p. 225.

4   *Portsmouth People*, December 2012, p. 3.

5   *Rule of St Benedict*, Prologue, line 21.

6   Pope Saint John Paul II, *From Subiaco shines a Beacon of Faith*, Rome, 7 July 1999.

7   *Portsmouth People*, December 2012, p. 9.

8   Ibid., p. 14.

9   A statement from the Bishop of Portsmouth, 14 January 2010, posted on CBCEW website.

10 Cormac Murphy-O'Connor, *An English Spring* (London: Bloomsbury, 2015), p. 116.

11 Cf. Brigitte Hoegemann, *Newman and Rome*, 23–4 (A pamphlet of the International Centre of Newman Friends first published in *John Henry Newman in His Time* (Oxford: Family Publications, 2007), pp. 61–81).

12 Peter Jennings (ed.), *Benedict XVI and Blessed John Henry Newman: The State Visit 2010, the Official Record*, p. 39.

13 Portsmouth Diocese, Pastoral Letter of Bishop Hollis, 7 March 2011.

14 Quoted in *Independent Catholic News*, 21 November 2011, <https://www.indcatholicnews.com/news/19353>, accessed 30 August 2024.

15 Quoted in *The Catholic Herald*, 31 May 2012.

16 *Portsmouth People*, December 2012, p. 18.

17 See <https://www.pierrebamin.com/bishop-emery/>, accessed 30 August 2024.

The Bishops of Bamenda

As we have seen, the Diocese of Portsmouth has a special link with the Archdiocese of Bamenda in Cameroon. This link was formally established in 1974, and in this short appendix I want to briefly consider this diocese and its bishops. In places where the Catholic Church is not sufficiently well established, it has apostolic prefectures, governed by an apostolic prefect who is the ordinary, often but not always a bishop, but not a diocesan bishop of that territory. The apostolic prefecture of Cameroon was established in 1890 and put under the administration of the Pious Society of Missions (the Pallotine Fathers). Father Henry Vieter was the first apostolic prefect.

In 1905, the prefecture was raised to the status of a vicariate, roughly equivalent to a diocese, under an apostolic vicar. In 1923, this vicariate was divided and the apostolic prefecture of Buea was formed, which in turn was promoted to an apostolic vicariate in 1939, and then in 1950 further promoted again to form the Diocese of Buea under its first diocesan bishop, Peter Rogan MHM. At that time, Bamenda was part of the Diocese of Buea.

In 1970, Pope Paul VI, by his Bull *Tametsi Christianarum*, detached part of the territory of the Diocese of Buea to form the Diocese of Bamenda. St Joseph's Church in Bamenda, originally a small chapel on a hill, established by the Mill Hill Missionaries, became the new cathedral. In 1982, there was further restructuring, by Pope Saint John Paul II; his Bull *Eo magis Ecclesia Catholica* raised the diocese to the dignity of a Metropolitan Archdiocese, and the same Bull established Buea, Kumbo and Mamfe as three suffragan dioceses.

The first Bishop of Bamenda was Bishop Paul Verdzekov, who became archbishop in 1982, when the diocese became an archdiocese. He was succeeded by Archbishop Cornelius Fontem Esau, who was in turn succeeded by Archbishop Andrew Nkea Fuanya in 2019.

Paul Verdzekov was born in Shisong on 22 January 1931. He was ordained priest on 20 December 1961. On 13 August 1970, he was appointed Bishop of Bamenda, and he was ordained bishop on 8 November by Bishop Julius Peeters MHM (Bishop of Buea) assisted by Bishop Yves-Joseph-Marie Plumey OMI (Garoua) and Bishop Pierre Célestin Nkou (Sangmélima).

When the diocese became an archdiocese, Verdzekov became archbishop. He retired in January 2006 and died in 2010 aged 79.

Archbishop Verdzekov was succeeded by Archbishop Cornelius Esau who was born in Mbetta, in southwest Cameroon on 2 July 1943, to Michael Esau and his wife Felicitas. He was ordained to the priesthood on 29 December 1971. He was appointed bishop of Kumbo in 1982 and was ordained in the open air near St Augustin's College in Kumbo by Archbishop Donato Squicciarni (1927–2006), at that time the apostolic nuncio to Cameroon, assisted by Bishop Paul Verdzekov (Bamenda) and Bishop Pius Suh Awa (Buea). He took the episcopal motto *Sermo tuus veritas est*, meaning "your word is truth". In 2004, Bishop Esau was appointed coadjutor bishop of Bamenda by Pope Saint John Paul II and was translated to the See in 2006. Esau made *ad limina* visits to Rome in 2006 and 2014.

Esau retired on 30 December 2019 and is currently the Bishop Emeritus of Bamenda.

Esau was succeeded by Andrew Fuanya Nkea, who was born on 26 August 1965. He studied at the seminary of St Thomas Aquinas in Bambui and was ordained priest for the diocese of Buea on 22 April 1992. On 23 August 2013, he was ordained coadjutor Bishop of Mamfe by Archbishop Piero Pioppo (titular of Torcello) assisted by Bishop Francis Lysinge (Mamfe) and Bishop Emmanuel Bushu (Buea). The following year, in 2014, he became the Bishop of Mamfe.

In 2019, he was appointed Archbishop of Bamenda and was installed in his new cathedral the following year, February 2020. Bishop Nkea has made peace and reconciliation the cornerstone of his episcopacy. Despite the dangers, he has condemned the abuses perpetrated by the army (particularly their involvement in the death of the Kenyan missionary

Cosmos Oboto Ondari), and he has encouraged "child-soldiers" to return to school. "Only a frank and sincere dialogue can lead to a lasting peace," he said.

There have been two auxiliary bishops in Bamenda. Between 2011 and 2016, Bishop Enuyehnyoh Nfon was auxiliary bishop. He was born on 11 February 1964 and ordained priest on 22 March 1991. He was ordained as titular bishop of Unizibira and served as auxiliary in Bamenda for five years before his appointment as Bishop of Kumba on 15 March 2016.

Between 2017 and 2021, Bishop Michael Bibi was auxiliary bishop in Bamenda. He was born on 28 July 1971 and ordained to the priesthood on 26 April 2000. On 24 January, he was appointed titular Bishop of Amudarsa and auxiliary bishop in Bamenda. He was ordained bishop on 25 March 2017 by Archbishop Esau, in St Joseph's Cathedral in Bamenda. On 25 January 2021, he was appointed as Bishop of Buea and installed in his new cathedral on 25 February 2021.

Bibliography

Bellinger, Dominic Aidan and Fletcher, Stella, *Princes of the Church* (Stroud: Sutton Publishing, 2001).

Burton, Edwin H. DD and Pollen, J. H. SJ (eds), *Lives of the English Martyrs*, vol. I (London: Longman, Green & Co., 1914).

Clarke, P., *Ryde to Rome* (Isle of Wight Catholic History Society, unpublished, 2003).

Congar, Yves, *My Journal of the Council*, tr. Mary John Ronayne OP and Mary Cecily Boulding OP (Collegeville, MN: Liturgical Press, 2012).

Dwyer, G., *Diocese of Portsmouth: Past and Present* (Portsmouth: Portsmouth Diocesan Centenary Committee, 1981).

Elder, Fraser, Gilfeather, Martin and Wilkie, George, *Always Winning* (Edinburgh: Mainstream Publishing Company, 2001).

Fontana, V. J. L., *Rebirth of Roman Catholicism in Portsmouth* (City of Portsmouth: Portsmouth Papers, 1989).

Fontana, V. J. L., *St John's Cathedral Portsmouth* (Norfolk: Jarrold Publishing, 2003).

Furnival, John and Knowles, Ann, *Archbishop Derek Worlock: His Personal Journey* (London: Geoffrey Chapman, 1998).

Gilroy, E., *Mary Potter* (London: CTS, 2010).

Greenacre, R. and Haselock, J., *The Sacrament of Easter* (Leominster: Gracewing, 1989, 1991).

Grehan, J. and Mace, M., *The Zulu War: Despatches from the Front* (Barnsley: Pen & Sword, 2013).

Heenan, J., *Not the Whole Truth* (London: Hodder & Stoughton, 1971).

Holland, Thomas, *For Better and for Worse* (Salford: Salford Diocese, 1989).

Houseley, C., *A History of the Catholic Church in Havant* (Havant: Bishop's Printers, 2000).

Jennings, Peter (ed.), *Benedict XVI and Blessed John Henry Newman: The State Visit 2010, the Official Record* (London: CTS, 2010).

Jennings, Peter and McCabe, Eamonn, *The Pope in Britain* (London: The Bodley Head, 1982).

Kelly, Kevin, *50 Years Receiving Vatican II* (Dublin: Columba Press, 2012).

Kenny, A., *A Path from Rome* (London: Sidgwick & Jackson, 1985).

Kloppenburg, Bonaventure, *Ecclesiology of Vatican II* (Chicago, IL: Franciscan Herald Press, 1974).

Longley, Clifford, *The Worlock Archive* (London: Geoffrey Chapman, 2000).

McDonald, A. and Karlsson C., *Venerable Mary Potter at Southsea Portsmouth* ('Little Company of Mary' booklet, unpublished, 2003).

Murphy-O'Connor, Cormac, *An English Spring* (London: Bloomsbury, 2015).

O'Connor, William, *Opus Dei: An Open Book* (Dublin: The Mercier Press, 1991).

Scantlebury, R. E., *The Catholic Story of the Isle of Wight* (Havant: Pelham, 1962).

Shrimpton Paul, *A Catholic Eton? Newman's Oratory School* (Leominster: Gracewing, 2005).

Straker, Barbara J., *St Saviour's R.C. Church and Community* (Isle of Wight: St Saviour's Church, 2001).

Walsh, Michael J., *The Westminster Cardinals* (London: Burns & Oates, 2008).

Whitehead, Kenneth, *History of the Somerset Light Infantry* (Somerset Light Infantry, 1961).

Williams, Michael E., *The Venerable English College, Rome* (Leominster: Gracewing, 1979, 2008).

Catechism of the Catholic Church (London: Geoffrey Chapman, 1994) (=CCC).

EU GPSR Authorized Representative:

LOGOS EUROPE, 9 rue Nicolas Poussin, 17000 La Rochelle, France

contact@logoseurope.eu

www.ingramcontent.com/pod-product-compliance
Ingram Content Group UK Ltd.
Pitfield, Milton Keynes, MK11 3LW, UK
UKHW020706260525
6080UKWH00038B/453